LESSONS *for* LIVING

VOLUME 2: EVANGELISM

EDITED BY

Niares A. Hunn, D.D., Ph.D.,
Natasha R. Williams, M.B.A.,
and Paul H. Evans, Sr., B.S.

WESTBOW
PRESS®
A DIVISION OF THOMAS NELSON
& ZONDERVAN

Scripture taken from the King James Version of the Bible.

WestBow Press books may be ordered through booksellers or by contacting:

WestBow Press
A Division of Thomas Nelson & Zondervan
1663 Liberty Drive
Bloomington, IN 47403
www.westbowpress.com
1 (866) 928-1240

ISBN: 978-1-5127-2510-0 (sc)
ISBN: 978-1-5127-2511-7 (e)

Library of Congress Control Number: 2015917471

Print information available on the last page.

WestBow Press rev. date: 1/14/2016

Contents

About The Editors

Bishop Paul H. Evans, Sr. is the Pastor of Grace Gospel Temple in St. Charles, MO and the father of three – Karen, Sheila, and Paul Jr. He began his ministry in 1966 at Lively Stone Church in St. Louis, MO and became the Pastor of Lively Stone Church in 1975 located in Mt. Vernon, IL. He has been married to Helen R. Evans since the 14th of June 1959. Bishop Evans is a graduate of Washington University in St. Louis, MO with a Bachelor's of Science degree in Sociology. Bishop Evans is the leader and vanguard behind the *"Lessons for Living"* publication along with his staff Natasha R. Williams, and Dr. Niares A. Hunn.

Natasha R. Williams is the mother of two – Constance and Andrew III and the wife of Elder Andrew S. Williams, Jr. since March 2008. She received a Bachelor's of Science degree in Biology (with a minor in Chemistry) from the University of Missouri-St. Louis and she is a graduate of the Pierre Laclede Honors College at the University of Missouri-St. Louis. Natasha has received a Master of Business Administration degree from Webster University, graduating with Graduate Academic Honors. She is a member of the Internationally-renowned American Society for Quality (ASQ) and has been certified through ASQ as a Six Sigma Black Belt, Six Sigma Green Belt, and Quality Process Analyst. Natasha is also a Member of Delta Mu Delta International Honors Society in Business.

Dr. Niares A. Hunn is the mother of three – Jonathan II, Joshua, and Jadon and the wife of Minister Jonathan W. Hunn, Sr. since January 1997. Dr. Hunn has received a Bachelor's of Arts in Criminal Justice and Sociology from St. Louis University, Masters of Theology from Logos Christian University, and Masters of Education in Instructional Technology from American Inter-Continental University (AIU), Doctor of Divinity from Christian Bible College, and is a graduate of Walden University with a Doctor of Philosophy in Educational Technology.

Lessons For Living
Contributing Writers

C. Jean Bembry
Maurice N. Bembry, Sr.
Barbara Brown
Deborah Burch
Wanda E. Burton
Dianne Campbell
Freddie I. Campbell
Luebertha Conner
Doris Davis
Johnny Davis
Helen R. Evans
Paul H. Evans, Sr.
Latunya Farr
Eugene Folks, Jr.
Sylvia Folks
Dr. Camesha Hill-Carter
Betty J. Hunn
Jonathan W. Hunn, II
Jonathan W. Hunn, Sr.
Niares A. Hunn
Savannah G. Jones
Tammy N. Jones
Karen Kessee
Terrence Kessee
Evelyn Ledford
Gerald W. Ledford, Jr.
Gerald W. Ledford, Sr.
Pamela Ledford
Sharonda N. Littleton
Donald Lowrance, Jr.

Theresa Lowrance
Barbara Rusan
Sharon L. Russell
Helen J. Thomas
Sandra D. Walker
Christopher Walls, Sr.
Sheila D. Walls
Andrew S. Williams, Jr.
Natasha R. Williams

Introduction

By Orlando and Karen Smith

The Lessons for Living series is designed to prepare students to deal with a complex, diverse, and ever-changing society. Our mission is to integrate faith and learning, providing exemplary academics, spiritual foundation, and skills to engage and transform the world. Our desire is that readers will be empowered to think holistically, reason analytically, and communicate persuasively, preparing them for a lifetime of growth in their careers, churches, and communities.

To ensure these outcomes are presented to the readers, we have designed a series that will:

1. Support the local facilitator of the curriculum with a series that will encourage attendance through the discussion questions and curriculum design.
2. Develop a thematic scheme outlining the course objectives and outcomes of each lesson.
3. Support annual professional development in order to receive a specified number of CEU's.
4. Demonstrate the ability to deliver classroom and/or online instruction effectively while meeting baseline standards.
5. Support students in achieving their highest, divine potential.

The above-mentioned criteria have been set forth and approved by each contributing writer. With this in mind, this curriculum is designed to provide a more profound appreciation of the theological aspects of the doctrine of evangelism deliberated from a systematic, historical, biblical, and practical perspective.

It is also our hope that individuals teaching this series will meet and understand at least 3 criteria: evangelism, instruction, and faith. Evangelism is used to win souls for God, instruction is used to provide Godly truth, and faith implementing what you know to be true. With these practices, the contemporary relevance of evangelism for the Christian life and the practice of ministry will be stressed.

Lessons For Living Poem

By Yolanda Newson

As we travel down the road of life, there are a few things we should understand;
The path was laid and the plan has been made and they're placed in God's hands.

We war neither with flesh nor blood, but with the spiritually wicked powers that be;
To understand how to defeat the enemy we must all get in our Bibles and read.

We must feed on the Word of God daily, for it will guide us on our way;
To live a holy, sanctified, and separated life until He returns for us one day.

UNIT 1: EVANGELISM AND MISSIONS

Lesson 1: What is Evangelism?

ACTS 1:1-8

By Jonathan W. Hunn, II

> *Key Verse: But ye shall receive power, after that the Holy Ghost is come upon you: and ye shall be witnesses unto me both in Jerusalem, and in all Judaea, and in Samaria, and unto the uttermost part of the earth (Acts 1:8).*

After completing this lesson, the learner will be able to:

1. Explain what evangelism is.
2. List steps to personal evangelism.
3. Value evangelism as an essential part of church growth.

In the Christian community, it has become popular to proclaim oneself a follower of Christ but never do His works. While we are all guilty of doing this at one time or another, it is essential that we do the task God has set before all of us. That means to prescribe and follow all that God has for us as we *walk in total holiness*. One thing that God has called us to do is to bring others into the Kingdom.

Through the years several methods of evangelism have been tried, used, and thrown out. Jesus has given us the perfect tool which He covers extensively with His disciples (the early apostles). In Acts 1:5-8 He speaks of the Spirit He shall send them to help guide them and witness (or evangelize) to the people of Jerusalem, all of Judea, Samaria, and the uttermost part of the earth. This is speaking of local evangelism to those that are of the Jewish descent. Jerusalem was the capital city of the kingdom of Judah (Judea) and Samaria was the capital city of the kingdom of Israel. Their kingdoms are similar to our states or territories. Thus, when the

3

Scripture speaks of all of Judea or Judah in verse 8, it means the whole state or the whole kingdom.

Indeed, evangelism is our way of spreading the Gospel of Jesus Christ to people and the parameters of the people to which they were to reach were clearly outlined in Acts 1:8 in which this lesson today will focus on Jerusalem and Samaria. Thus, evangelism is proclaiming the gospel publicly or by preaching. It can also include sharing your personal testimony as the Apostle Paul has demonstrated in scripture (Acts 22:3-5). Normally this act includes being a strong advocate for the cause to which you are proclaiming and being zealous. Notice how the dictionary does not once ever state that you must be limited to a certain location, city, state, or country to minister to others. That would be described as missionary work; which in itself is a completely different type of ministry. Although for now, we will focus on evangelism and different ways to evangelize.

The Bible lists countless ways to evangelize people, but we want to pursue ways to this current generation. It may come as a surprise to you that some of these things that you were taught as a part of your original foundation as a part of salvation are still important and should never lose its "appeal". Evangelism and church growth is still vital to reach the lost and to expand the Kingdom of God. One evangelistic ministry that is vibrant and prevalent today is the Awana Club (*A*pproved *W*orkmen *A*re *N*ot *A*shamed) which is a globally-sponsored organization founded to get children and teens alike excited to learn about the Gospel of Jesus Christ. Awana has a pre-designed curriculum that includes lessons, discussion, and games, with plenty of space for personal testimony and one-on-one work with the students. It is an excellent program (I have personally participated in it) and has many representatives to work with you to help you get started.

A similar program, although at the same time different, is scouting. Scouting in the USA is an individualized program that separates individuals based on gender (Girl Scouts or Boy Scouts) and allows one to learn outdoor skills, cooking, and how to become a functioning member of society. Scouting is also greatly supported by many religious organizations; furthermore, it allows you to be supported by leaders that are like-minded with you in faith. Scouting is a very diverse program which allows one to join and participate quite easily. This is another way you can find out about evangelism through scouting by checking with your local church and/or community to learn how they help sponsor Boy Scout Troops.

Lastly, since we have covered two global programs that you can implement in your church ministry to evangelize the lost in your community, there are also things you can do to personally evangelize individuals. These are simple things that you can do each day such as:

1. Pray for those who are not Christians
2. Share your faith with current friends and build relationships
3. Talk with those who appear to be spiritually thirsty
4. Take time to talk to strangers and welcome impromptu conversations to share your faith
5. Knock on doors to leave tracts or invite others to church
6. Community Outreach Activities (Back to School Events, Summer Vacation Bible School, Summer Christian Camp Counselor, AWANA Clubs, Boy/Girl Scouts, College Outreach Ministries)

All of these are programs you can either volunteer to serve with or launch and coordinate at your local assembly. This lesson has provided information such as defining evangelism, covered basic steps to personal evangelism, and provided ideas on how to get evolved with evangelism. Our hope now is that you would implement this knowledge into your personal witness and that you will be empowered and enabled to be a witness for Jesus Christ.

Discussion Questions

1. Why is evangelism an important part of church growth?
2. How can an individual get involved in evangelism? Does a person have to evangelize to be saved?
3. Is evangelism a part of making disciples? If so, then how?

Thought to Remember

Our desire should be for others to be saved.

Lesson 2: What is Missions?

MARK 16:15-20; 1 PETER 2:9
By Sharon L. Russell

Key Verse: And he said unto them, Go ye into all the world, and preach the gospel to every creature (Mark 16:15).

After completing this lesson, students will be able to:

1. Identify the purpose of missions.
2. Recall leadership qualities of being a successful mission worker.
3. Explain the different types of missions work.

Missions can be defined as a person accepting the vocation of sharing their faith with others in the world. God has given us a charge as Christians to go out and spread the gospel. We are to be witnesses to our friends, family, co-workers, and strangers and tell of the goodness of Jesus. We must understand that mission work is carried out in numerous places, and in different ways, involving all ethnic backgrounds, nations, and cultures.

Luke 10:2 says, *Therefore, said he unto them, The harvest truly is great, but the labourers are few: pray ye therefore the Lord of the harvest, that he would send forth labourers into his harvest.* We are living in a lost and dying world. The number of souls that need saving is GREAT; however, there are few that are willing to go and spread the good news. We have to stay prayerful and seek the Lord that He may lead and guide us in what He wants us to do so that our labor is not in vain.

Discussion Questions

1. Do you possess the leadership qualities to be a successful mission worker?
2. What opportunities do you see in the United States to do mission work?
3. Are you willing to go?

Thought to Remember

Be not afraid of what God has commissioned you to do. Every day is an opportunity to be a witness to someone about the goodness of Jesus! *Wherefore the rather, brethren, give diligence to make your calling and election sure: for if ye do these things, ye shall never fall* (2 Peter 1:10).

Lesson 3: Peter the Evangelist

Acts 2:16-20; Acts 10
By Sharon L. Russell

Key Verse: And it shall come to pass in the last days, saith God, I will pour out of my Spirit upon all flesh: and your sons and your daughters shall prophesy, and your young men shall see visions, and your old men shall dream dreams (Acts 2:17).

After completing this lesson, students will be able to:

1. Identify the key characteristics that Peter possessed as an Evangelist.
2. Recall the different types of Evangelistic work that Peter performed.
3. Express the meaning and purpose of an Evangelist.

An evangelist is an individual that has accepted the vocation as a minister of the gospel with a specialization in revivals. The Bible tells us that Peter was an evangelist; a fisherman of men to win souls to Christ as he proclaimed the Gospel (spread the good news). Peter had a close relationship with Jesus. In order to be an evangelist, we have to have a close relationship with Jesus. We have to go in unfamiliar places, to reach the lost. We may be afraid at times, but we have to trust in the Lord and know that God has not given us a spirit of fear. If we allow the Lord to order our steps, He will not lead us to failure. We have to be like Peter:

- Willing to go,
- Willing to follow,
- Willing to be taught.

9

Discussion Questions

1. In what ways was Peter effective in reaching the lost?
2. What characteristics did Peter possess as a successful evangelist?
3. Is anything keeping you from winning souls to Christ?

Thought to Remember

We should always be willing to go, willing to follow, and willing to be taught. We must stay open and receptive to the Lord - Then said I, Here am I; send me (Isaiah 6:8)!

Lesson 4: Paul the Missionary

EPHESIANS 3:1-2; ROMANS 1:5
By Andrew S. Williams, Jr. and Natasha R. Williams

Key Verse: By whom we have received grace and apostleship, for obedience to the faith among all nations, for his name (Romans 1:5).

After completing this lesson, the learner will be able to:

1. Appreciate the correlation between mission, missionary, and evangelism.
2. Explain why we need to have the same zeal as Paul did, in winning souls for the Lord.
3. Recognize that evangelism is not an option.

Before we can understand how and why Paul was so effective in bringing souls to Christ during his missionary journeys, let's begin by taking a look at the type of man that he was. Saul (prior to his conversion on the Damascus Road, after which he is referred to as "Paul") was a bold and radical Jew, born in the city of Tarsus, the capital of the Roman province Cilicia. He was passionate about what he believed, and prior to his conversion, he believed that he was doing the will of God when he persecuted Jewish Christians who were not loyal to or felt that they had to be subject to Jewish laws and beliefs. Various scriptures tell us how Paul zealously and antagonistically persecuted the church:

Acts 8:3 – As for Saul, he made havoc of the church, entering into every house, and haling men and women committed them to prison.

Acts 22:4 - And I persecuted this way unto the death, binding and delivering into prisons both men and women.

Acts 26:11 - And I punished them oft in every synagogue, and compelled them to blaspheme; and being exceedingly mad against them, I persecuted them even unto strange cities.

Galatians 1:13 - For ye have heard of my conversation in time past in the Jews' religion, how that beyond measure I persecuted the church of God, and wasted it:

Philippians 3:6 - Concerning zeal, persecuting the church; touching the righteousness which is in the law, blameless.

While on his way to Damascus to capture and bind believers to bring them back to Jerusalem to be jailed, Paul had a dramatic encounter with the Lord Jesus Christ, which changed the course of his life forever (see Acts 9:3-6). This "face-to-face" encounter with the Lord Jesus Christ turned Paul 180 degrees. He now understood that he had been persecuting the Lord when he thought all along that he had been doing His will. The church was truly a people that belonged to the Lord and the Lord let Paul know that He was not pleased. But once the Lord revealed Himself to Paul, what was Paul's first reply? He asked Jesus, "Lord, what do You want me to do?" He immediately sought God's will and direction as he now understood that what he was doing was not God's will. He persecuted the very One he thought he'd pleased by his actions. The Lord told him to go into Damascus and he would receive the details of his assignment. Webster's Dictionary defines *missionary* as "a person undertaking a mission and especially a religious mission" and describes *mission* as "a task or job that someone is given to do". After his Damascus Road experience, Paul was visited by Ananias who gave him the details of his mission. It says in Acts 22:14-16:

[14] And he said, The God of our fathers hath chosen thee, that thou shouldest know his will, and see that Just One, and shouldest hear the voice of his mouth. [15] For thou shalt be his witness unto all men of what thou hast seen and heard . [16] And now why tarriest thou? arise, and be baptized, and wash away thy sins, calling on the name of the Lord.

Acts 9:20 says that "And straightway (suddenly, directly, instantaneously, right away) he preached Christ in the synagogues, that he is the Son of God." He began to take that same zeal, drive, and passion that he had prior to his conversion and began to relentlessly preach Jesus wherever he went. Acts 9:22 says, "But Saul increased the more in strength, and confounded the Jews which dwelt at Damascus, proving that this is the very Christ." Paul was not to keep what the Lord had done in his life to himself. He was to be a witness for the Lord, commissioned by God to share Him wherever he went without fear or reservation (Romans 1:5). He was indeed a missionary, a man who had been given a job to do and he pursued it with all he had.

Discussion Questions

1. What was Paul's response when the Lord revealed Himself to him on the Damascus Road? Should our response to the Lord's call be the same?
2. How did Paul approach the mission that God had given to Him?
3. When Paul asked the Lord who He was in Acts 9:5a on the Damascus Road, the Lord said, "I am Jesus, whom thou persecutest". What is the meaning of this, if the scriptures also say that Paul persecuted Christian believers?

Thought to Remember

We often think of missionaries as Christians being sent overseas to share the Gospel, but there is fertile ground all around us. Ask the Lord to guide you and be obedient to Him as you share the Gospel of Jesus Christ with others!

Lesson 5: Philip the Deacon and Evangelist

ACTS 6:1-7; ACTS 8:1-40
By Gerald W. Ledford, Jr. and Pamela Ledford

Key Verse: Then Philip went down to the city of Samaria, and preached Christ unto them. And the people with one accord gave heed unto those things which Philip spake, hearing and seeing the miracles which he did (Acts 8:5-6).

After completing this lesson, the learner will be able to:

1. Describe the office of a deacon in the early church.
2. Recognize the importance of Philip's role in spreading the gospel as he became an evangelist.
3. Appraise the potency of evangelism to the Body of Christ.

Before we can begin to look at Philip the Deacon, we must first know the background on how the office of a deacon came about. The office of a deacon in a church setting began in Acts 6, when the apostles selected seven men to supervise the church ministry to the needs of its widows. It was important to select men who had a reputation for being trustworthy, honest, and faithful because they were going to be entrusted with finances to purchase food, and distribute it properly.

Also, it was very important that the seven men were full of the Holy Ghost, as such work would require a great amount of wisdom and leading of the Spirit. Philip was one of the seven chosen by the leaders of the church including the congregation. He along with the

15

other six who were chosen, was consistent with their confession of faith.

Now we will look at the role of Philip as an evangelist. An *Evangelist* (Greek, announcer of good news), was generally used for someone who proclaimed The Gospel in places where it was previously unknown - such work becoming known as evangelism. Philip was one of the seven deacons (Acts 6:5-6) and was also an evangelist (Acts 21:8). After the martyrdom of Stephen, Philip left Jerusalem, which started his ministry of evangelism. Philip took the Gospel of Jesus Christ to Samaria, where many believed and were baptized.

The Bible says that many miracles and signs were done. After this had taken place, the angel of the Lord directed Philip to go south to the road that went from Jerusalem into Gaza. We can compare his response with the unquestioning obedience of Abraham. We know that faith in God means being ready to move, without explanation. Because Philip obeyed, this brought him in contact with an Ethiopian eunuch of great influence. As the Ethiopian was reading Scripture, Philip was directed by the Spirit to join him, and the truth of Scripture (Jesus, the righteous sufferer, crucified and risen again, has won the victory over sin and death, and now repentance and forgiveness of sins are available in His name) brought that man to faith in Christ, after which Philip baptized him. After this event, Philip continues his witness and preaching of the Gospel of Jesus Christ.

Discussion Questions

1. What were the requirements of the deacon?
2. Should the requirements of the deacon be the requirement for any job God had called us to do in the church?
3. How did Philip and Abraham respond when God told them to go?

Thought to Remember

Every Holy Ghost-filled believer is called to share the gospel. We should be compelled to speak the Good News to any that will listen. As the ones sent by God (that's us), we should be ready to "tell the story" to the world.

UNIT 2: GOD COMMANDS US

Lesson 1: It's Time to Work

MARK 9:37-38
By Dr. Camesha Hill-Carter

Key Verse: Whosoever shall receive one of such children in my name, receiveth me: and whosoever shall receive me, receiveth not me, but him that sent me. And John answered him, saying, Master, we saw one casting out devils in thy name, and he followeth not us: and we forbad him, because he followeth not us (Mark 9:37-38).

After completing this lesson, the learner will be able to:

1. Describe how he/she shares the love of Jesus with others.
2. Identify and demonstrate the love of Jesus in their daily lives.
3. Analyze how to share God's love with those of a different faith and background.

In Cleveland, Ohio, Tamir Rice[1], playing at a park, was fatally shot by police who assumed that his toy air gun was real, without doing an investigation prior to shooting him. Nine-year-old Jamyla Bolden[2] was gunned down while she was doing her homework on her mother's bed by an unknown gunman in Ferguson, Missouri. Numerous deaths of young people infiltrate our media stream and everywhere we look, children are being brutally abused, neglected and unwanted. Some of those in the African-American population states that it is up to African-Americans to help their communities[3]. Other schools of thought are of the mindset that this war on children is a global epidemic to which all that is willing to help can and should[4].

In Africa, there is a call and response greeting given to those who pass by villages throughout the land. The passer-by shouts, "How are the children?" The response is "The children are well![5]"

21

This lets the passerby know that the village is healthy and the village will not end up in bitter ruin due to the lack of sustainability of the next generation.

In close parallel, the kingdom of God, here on Earth, is under attack. People are falling away from the church due to unbelief, loss, hurt and pain. Many believe that they have done so much wrong that there is no possible way that they may enter into heaven. Others feel that if I am my brother's keeper (Genesis 4:9), and is it then my responsibility to go above and beyond the call of duty to help someone who doesn't want to be helped? We, as Christians, should not hinder anyone who wants to come to Christ or do the work of Christ. Instead of doing nothing or pointing the finger at those who do, saying that their actions are not right, Jesus eloquently shares his thoughts through Mark 9:37-38: *37 "Whoever welcomes one of these little children in my name welcomes me; and whoever welcomes me does not welcome me but the one who sent me." 38"Teacher," said John, "we saw someone driving out demons in your name and we told him to stop, because he was not one of us."*

To illustrate this point further, in verse 37, Jesus was actually surrounded by little children. The children came to Jesus from all around. I could imagine Jesus with welcoming arms to hug, to love, to embrace, to approve, to equip, to honor, to care. If God uses us to show His love toward people then we are to welcome the unsaved, the unchurched, and the unlearned in the same manner as Jesus did. In James 2, we are warned about judging people by their appearance. We should accept everyone based upon their character, who they are and not what they possess. This makes it easier for us to share the gospel of Jesus Christ to all regardless of status, creed, color, gender or orientation. We must welcome all to Christ. Whether the individual hears or forbears, there has been a person to give them the opportunity to have Jesus as their personal Lord and Savior. Is not that truly our job as saints of the most high God?

On the same token, in verse 38, Jesus rebukes the disciples because there were people casting out devils in Jesus' name. This was not a harsh rebuke, but a thought-provoking rebuke to have the disciples look deeper at this scene before judgment is passed. How can one cast out devils in my name and turn around and not be one of God's chosen? This instance, in Scripture, shows that if you believe on the Lord Jesus then you shalt be saved.

This scene also shows that it doesn't matter your denomination or affiliation, if you believe Jesus then you believe in Jesus' saving power. These people had enough faith to cast out demons in the name of Jesus' without being in the camp of the disciples. Who are we to judge and say that because they are not of our flock they are not a part of the Kingdom? Is there a twinge of jealousy there because others are doing the work you are to be doing? Is there an overwhelming sense of guilt because you have cluttered your time with busy work and not the work of Christ? Let's face it! We are all guilty, and we are all busy! Let us get to work and find one person a day to minister to about the love of Jesus Christ. Let us not look with a side-eye to those who approach us, wanting to know more about the God you serve. Let us not get weary in well doing because in due season we shall reap if we faint not. Saints of God, it is time to work!

Discussion Questions

1. How would you approach someone about the love of Jesus?
2. Janey was raised in the occult. Her body is filled with elaborate tattoos of death, killing and Satanic worship. She wanted to learn more about your "religion". How would you approach this situation?
3. How are you going to share the love of Jesus everyday?

A Thought to Remember

Regardless of who you are, we are all working toward the cause of Christ, which is salvation for the lost and redemption for the saved.

Niares A. Hunn, D.D., Ph.D., Natasha R. Williams, M.B.A., and Paul H. Evans, Sr., B.S.

Notes

"Tamir Rice report: No proof officer warned … - CNN.com." 2015. 26 Aug. 2015 <http://www.cnn.com/2015/06/13/us/tamir-rice-report/

"Jamyla Bolden funeral information released; reward increased." 2015. 26 Aug. 2015 <http://fox2now.com/2015/08/24/jamyla-bolden-funeral-information-released-reward-increased/>

"Education Secretary Arne Duncan Visits Ferguson - The Root." 2015. 26 Aug. 2015 <http://www.theroot.com/articles/culture/2015/02/education_secretary_arne_duncan_visits_ferguson.html>

"Will Nigeria's abducted schoolgirls ever be found … - BBC.com." 2014. 26 Aug. 2015 <http://www.bbc.com/news/world-africa-27293418>

"And how are the children?" - The Registry." 2012. 26 Aug. 2015 <https://www.the-registry.org/Portals/0/Documents/Credentials/Administrator/Documents/And%20how%20are%20the%20children.pdf>

Lesson 2: Jesus Gives the Command

MATTHEW 28:19-20
By Dr. Camesha Hill-Carter

Key Verse: And that repentance and remission of sins should be preached in his name among all nations, beginning at Jerusalem. And ye are witnesses of these things (Luke 24:47-48).

After completing this lesson, the learner will be able to:

1. Employ and obey the command to go.
2. Outline a strategy to make disciples.
3. Recognize what to say as we disciple others.

Go! Go? Go. Every human being understands the pure essence of the word "go". As shown in the aforementioned sentence, regardless of what punctuation you put behind go, go denotes a forward movement of some kind. When I was younger, if I didn't want to get in trouble for fighting again, I would tell the other person "You betta' Go!" When I was a little older, the "go" became a question mark at the end because I was leaving my family and had questioned the move to college - go? Finally, as I have matured, go, as a command, means that my steps are sure (Psalm 37:23) as I follow God's plan for my life. Sometimes, when I go, I have a perfect plan but many other times, I get very frustrated because I have no clue as to what I need to do. Trusting in God and knowing that you are in blood covenant with Jesus (Mark 14:24), go in holy boldness (Hebrews 10:19-25) regardless of what the day may bring to you[4].

Similarly, as a follower of Jesus, we are commanded to go into the entire world and tell of the goodness of Jesus. In Matthew 28:19-20, Jesus gives the disciples the Great Commission. We have always known to tell others about Jesus but how to get it done has always been a mystery. In verse 19, Jesus tells the disciples to "Therefore go and make disciples of all nations, baptizing them in the name of the Father and of the Son and of the Holy Spirit. In reading this, Jesus, through the command, tells his disciples to" go and make". As a believer we are faced with the how of doing that. Let's clear this up a bit. You have the essential plan for salvation - hear the gospel, believe the gospel, repent of your sins, be filled with the Holy Spirt, and commit to obey and live for Jesus. Every situation is different. Your only job is to "go and make". Everything is done after the people become followers of Christ. The most important step in the following Jesus' command is "go and make".

The second part of the 19th verse and the entire 20th verse occur only after the profession of faith. 19b – "baptizing them in the name of the Father and of the Son and of the Holy Spirit" and 20 – "teaching them to obey everything I have commanded you. And surely I am with you always, to the very end of the age." This charge is to the leaders and workers of the house of God. I was once told, "You can't scale a fish you haven't caught." This saying was in reference to bringing in souls to the Lord. Until a person commits their ways to Christ, the actions within these verses cannot be performed. Once a person commits, then the clergy can baptize and teach. Surely, a person can be taught before baptism. Salvation is not achieved until the confession. Once the confession is made then Jesus becomes the vindicator (1 John 2:1) of those who have confessed Christ. Jesus is with those who have done as He commanded. Without this system in place, the cause of Christ dying for our sins will be null and void because there will be no one learning about his goodness.

Discussion Questions

1. Name three places you can go and compel men to come to Christ locally, regionally, nationally, internationally.

2. Why are repentance for those that get baptized and teaching them so that we make them become disciples and followers of Jesus Christ both necessary?
3. Chena wants to know more about the Lord. She attends Sunday School, Bible Study, and Morning Worship. She occasionally attends a prayer meeting. Chena has not confessed Christ. You have noticed it, but you don't want to pressure her to confess Christ at your church. What should you do?

Thought to Remember

It is not in the style or the manner in which you obey, just obey – Go.

Lesson 3: Jesus Has Guaranteed Our Success

John10:16; Psalm 126: 5-6
By Dr. Camesha Hill-Carter

> *Key Verse: He that goeth forth and weepeth, bearing precious seed, shall doubtless come again with rejoicing, bringing his sheaves with him (Psalm 126:6).*

After completing this lesson, the learner will be able to:

1. Discover that fear is from Satan and that God has guaranteed our success.
2. Model complete trust in Jesus as He works in your life.
3. Describe Jesus' successful discipleship plan.

What if I told you that you could not fail (Luke 1:37)? What if I told you that God is excited that you prosper and be in good health (3 John 1:2)? What if I told you that God wanted to bless you a 1,000 times more (Deuteronomy 1:11)? The blessings of the Lord are yea and amen (2 Corinthians 1:20). The blessing of the Lord maketh [you] rich and add no sorrow to it (Proverbs 10:22). Do you really believe that you can do all things through Christ that strengthens you (Philippians 4:13)? Yes, you can have whatever you say (Proverbs 18:12)!

Elvina Hall penned the song "Jesus Paid It All.[1]" The chorus of the verse states, *"Jesus paid it all. All to Him I owe. Sin has left its crimson stain. He washed it white as snow."* This shows us that Jesus took our sins to the cross and paid a ransom for our salvation (Romans 1:16); all of our sins - Jews and Gentiles - those who knew Him and those who will come to know Him. Jesus says in John 10:16, *"I have other sheep that are not of this sheep pen. I must bring them also. They too will listen to my voice, and there shall be one flock and one shepherd."* Have you been blessed by someone who doesn't look like you, talk like you, or act like you? Have you ever been given a compliment by a total and complete stranger? Haven't you blessed someone you don't even know? As soon as God drops it in your spirit to bless someone, you go and do it. That is why Jesus is letting you know that there are sheep that are not of this fold that God has orchestrated for you to cross paths to get to your desired outcome (Jeremiah 29:11). Who wouldn't serve a God like that? A God that has provided a sacrifice for our sin, a God who has paid it all and a God who has guaranteed our success!

Subsequently, Jesus has guaranteed our success, but we must walk out the plan God has for our lives. My three-year-old does not understand that there are boundaries he cannot cross at this time due to his age. His understanding is limited and he is not aware of potential dangers that can jeopardize his safety. In a like manner, God knows the right timing for us to have our blessings. If we get the blessing too early, we may not be ready for it and the blessing can do us more harm than good because of our lack of understanding. God will protect us. Holding fast to our faith will allow us to rest in the Lord. The psalmist says in Psalm 126 5-6: *5 Those who sow in tears will reap with songs of joy. 6 He who goes out weeping, carrying seed to sow, will return with songs of joy, carrying sheaves with him.* Jesus endured the cross, death, and the grave (Hebrews 12:2). He rose up with resurrection power that through Him we might be saved (Ephesians 2:8). Jesus has paid it all[2]. Now we have to have the faith to endure love, life, and loss (Hebrews 11:1). Because our steps are ordered by the Lord (Psalm 37:23) we will endure the hard times as soldiers (2 Timothy 2:3). We will have faith the size of a mustard seed (Matthew 17:20), when things don't go our way or the Lord is protecting us from ourselves (Psalm 121). We will not get weary in well doing because Jesus has guaranteed our success (Galatians 6:9).

Notes:

1. "Jesus Paid it All - Lyrics and Story Behind the Hymn." 2012. 31 Aug. 2015 <http://www.christianity.com/church/church-history/timeline/1801-1900/this-hymn-was-more-than-a-coincidence-11630381.html>

2. "Jesus Paid it All - Lyrics and Story Behind the Hymn." 2012. 31 Aug. 2015 <http://www.christianity.com/church/church-history/timeline/1801-1900/this-hymn-was-more-than-a-coincidence-11630381.html>

Discussion Questions

1. Why do we fear the future even though we know Jesus has guaranteed our success?
2. What can you do to trust Jesus' complete work in your life more?
3. Did you know that God has given you the desires of your heart? You just have to research and plan on how to do it. Often we have fear or feel it is too late for us to accomplish our dreams. List three things you need to give up today in order to walk out the plan of God for your life.

Thought to Remember

Jesus has already guaranteed your success. The only person who stops you from having all that God has for you is you.

Lesson 4: Commanded to Teach Jesus, the Only Savior

ACT 4:10-21; JOHN 14:6
By Dr. Camesha Hill-Carter

> *Key Verse: Neither is there salvation in any other: for there is none other name under heaven given among men, whereby we must be saved (Acts 4:12).*

After completing this lesson, the learner will be able to:

1. Examine why we are commanded to teach salvation only comes through Jesus.
2. Tell your testimony about Jesus saving power.
3. Explain why Jesus is the way, truth, and the life.

In today's society, we believe that there are so many things that can save our lives. We take medicines to help systems in our bodies so that we can be saved from dying from a disease. We put on our seatbelts to be saved from being thrown from the car. We get a good education so that we can be saved from poverty. We are always looking for safety and comfort in things, ideas, places and people. All of these things are temporal. People, places, things and ideas will pass away. You will only become a new creature once you confess Christ as your personal Lord and Savior. How does one get there? How does one find safety and comfort in God? It is done through the teachings that Jesus Christ is the only Savior.

Often times, the Bible is taught through opinion. This is parallel to the Pharisees and the Sadducees of the time. These teachers represent the Bible taught through the eyes of the law and not through the eyes of grace in Christ. In Acts 4: 10-21, Peter and

31

John stand before the Sanhedrin council after healing the man at the gate Beautiful. Peter and John, through trials and tribulations, boldly told about faith in God through the resurrection of Jesus Christ, that it is through Christ we have salvation. Bewildered, the Sanhedrin began to murmur because of the boldness of Peter and John as they spoke about Jesus, crucified and resurrected to save. In essence, Peter and John marveled the Sanhedrin by telling them this," *19 Judge for yourselves whether it is right in God's sight to obey you rather than God. 20 For we cannot help speaking about what we have seen and heard.*" At this point, how could the Sanhedrin hold them accountable? This lets us know, that Jesus is the only name by which man can be saved in the natural and the spiritual.

In John 14:6, Jesus gives us simple instruction on why he is the only savior. **6** Jesus saith unto him, I am the way, the truth, and the life: no man cometh unto the Father, but by me. The path to peace, love, understanding, perfect will, destiny, casting away of cares are all in the Way, the Truth, and The Life. Jesus knows the way. He is the way. He has shown us the way. He has shown us how to resist temptation. He has shown us how to prayer for those who despitefully use us. He has shown us how to stand when the world is against you. He has shown us that there is a place for us in heaven. He is the Truth. Every time you call on the name of Jesus, He answers. There is no other name that is above the name of Jesus. He is the standard to which we measure and judge our lives. He who knew no sin took sin to the cross on our behalf because he was already slain before the foundation of the Earth. The prophecy had to be fulfilled - the Truth. Jesus is the Life. In Him, Jesus, we live, breathe and have our being. It is in Him, we go from death to life. It is Him that is acquainted with all our infirmities. He is our lifeline to God because He is our advocate. He is the reason why grace and mercy follows us. This is why we are commanded to teach Jesus, the only Savior.

Discussion Questions

1. Why do you think we are commanded to teach Jesus as the only Savior?
2. Why is it important to tell your testimony about the goodness of Jesus?
3. Jesus is the way, the truth, and the life. What does that mean to you?

Thought to Remember

None come to the Father but by me- Jesus.

UNIT 3: FULFILLING THE COMMAND

Lesson 1: Empowered to Fulfill

ACTS 1:1-8
By Eugene Folks, Jr. and Sylvia Folks

Key Verse: For John truly, baptized with water; but ye shall be baptized with the Holy Ghost not many days hence (Acts 1:5).

After completing this lesson, the learner will be able to:

1. Define the word disciple.
2. Identify the steps to become a disciple.
3. Discover the mission of Christ's disciples.

During the three-year ministry of Jesus, He was everything to His disciples, as He helped them face and deal with any circumstance that came their way. As long as Jesus walked, talked, preached and taught His disciples, they had the power source in their midst and at their disposal. As part of His ministry, one of Jesus' main tasks was to get His disciples to automatically plug into His power, for every challenge. In the final months of His ministry, Jesus rehearsed with His disciples all that He had taught them, as He continued to tell them that He had to go away. One day, He sent them out two-by-two on a trial run, with power and authority. There was no better way to administer the most important test that would change mankind, while building confidence in His disciples and giving them a taste of the Holy Spirit that will come to their rescue later. They were armed and ready with all they were taught. They had plugged into Jesus, the never-ending power source and finally had an opportunity to test it and build their confidence. Jesus had done all that was necessary to train up a group of normal everyday men (Disciples), who He left to continue His ministry, by being witnesses of the love, character, power, truth, life, way and miracles of Jesus. Their newly adopted mission also included exploiting and compelling society at large to repent for their sin, be saved by the Savior, and renew themselves by the transforming power of Christ, the One Who was, Who is, and Who is forever more.

Thousands of years have passed since the recruitment and training of the first 12 disciples of Jesus and here we are, decedents in the 21st century. God is the same yesterday, today and forever more and He sits on heaven's throne today. God sent Jesus, His only Son, to demonstrate firsthand acts of servitude, caring, compassion, unconditional love, use of divine power and authority, needful ministry to each other and to the masses, etc... And now, Jesus currently sits at the right hand of God. Jesus is watching everyone who claims to be His disciples and one day He plans to pay a return visit.

In the meantime, while waiting on His return, we who profess to be Christian disciples of Jesus have an individual mission to accomplish. We can rest assured that if we put all that we have into the work of Jesus, He will surely empower us to fulfill whatever task we set out to accomplish. Ultimately, we who are disciples are empowered to fulfill the "Great Commission" left by Christ. We are empowered with power, strength and authority of Christ, to proclaim the Gospel, unto repentance, salvation, eternal life and the making of disciples. What must we do? We must first become a disciple. Then we must "Go" and make other disciples. We don't have to look or go too far, because the community in need is only one block away, in all directions. Making disciples is not easy by any stretch of the imagination, but because we are empowered by Christ, the Holy Spirit will provide the comfort needed. Disciples of Christ must facilitate a continual discipleship process, by prayer, proclaiming and applying the word of God and by personal testimony. Disciples of Christ must know, believe, trust and never forget that Jesus, through His Holy Spirit, is present and available during every step of the way, until He returns.

Discussion Questions

1. When you hear the word "disciple", what is the first thought that comes to mind and why?
2. How do we become "disciples of Christ"?
3. What is the mission of "disciples of Christ"?

Thought to Remember

Whoever makes the claim to be a follower of Christ has much work to do, according to the God-given gift within them.

Lesson 2: Preach the Word

ISAIAH 61:1; LUKE 4:14-20
By Eugene Folks, Jr. and Sylvia Folks

> *Key Verse: The Spirit of the Lord is upon me, because he hath anointed me to preach the gospel to the poor; he hath sent me to heal the brokenhearted to preach deliverance to the captives, and recovering of sight to the blind, to set at liberty them that bruised, to preach the acceptable year of the Lord (Luke 4:18-19).*

After completing this lesson, the learner will be able to:

1. Distinguish between a called minister and a lay person's witness.
2. Identify the qualifications of Jesus' disciples.
3. Analyze the role of the Holy Spirit and God's call to proclaim the gospel.

When we think of the word "preach", we think of a pastor or other preacher proclaiming "what thus says the Lord." The dictionary states that the word preach means "to make a public speech in a church or a public place about religion, to deliver a sermon, or to write and speak about a topic in an affirming manner." Preaching is also speaking about a topic that is necessary or something good so that the hearers behave the right way. Depending on how these definitions are interpreted, there is a great probability and possibility that the word preach is not solely connected to a pastor or preacher. In other words, they fit the résumé of any person, especially religious, who is not afraid to speak and/or write what is righteous.

Today's scripture is Luke's written account about the time that the resurrected Jesus joins His disciples, during their discussions after His death and burial. They had now learned about Jesus not being found at His burial site. When Jesus, who had become a stranger to them, made Himself apparent, they had a feeling that it was Him, but in their natural minds they doubted. The disciples would have never believed that Jesus was alive unless they could see and touch Him for themselves. They had forgotten what Jesus told them would take place. The Scripture says that Jesus opened their minds to clearly see what He had proclaimed to them, on more than one occasion, about His last days with them and what they must do after His departure. At this point, the requirement was simple. Jesus told them that when He goes home to His Father's house, that they must continue proclaiming who He is, by explaining, preaching, teaching, lecturing and by whatever else it takes to tell all nations that repentance and forgiveness must be asked in His name. The Bible says that at the name of Jesus, every knee shall bow and every tongue shall confess that Jesus Christ is Lord. Jesus provided lasting instructions and directions to His disciples about their way ahead and He prompted them to be ready to receive the comforting Helper that He will send back to help them. Jesus assured the disciples that they were capable witnesses, who must continually tell everyone the story of Jesus.

That brings us to the point of the matter, in verses 47-48. Jesus was talking to regular working class fishermen and relentless tax collectors. One point to consider is that all of His disciples were ordained to proclaim or preach Him. These men had flaws and faults, but Jesus didn't mind their flaws. They did not possess ministry résumés or ministry bios; nor, were they saving certificates of license or ministry ordination. The true ordaining source for the proclamation of the Gospel is the Holy Spirit. These simple men had been called from the darkness of the world's way into the marvelous light of God's spirituality. Jesus chose them to learn of Him and then He sent them into the world to keep His story alive

41

and fresh. The only condition required of the disciples then and of us today is for every believer to speak boldly and accurately, as a representative of Jesus. The Word of God must be proclaimed to continuously reveal the one and only Savior of the world, who paid the cost and paved the way, unto eternal life, but only by way of repentance of sin and forgiveness unto salvation.

Discussion Questions

1. Did Jesus choose His disciples because of who they were or who they were not? Choose one and explain.
2. Explain the meaning of Ministry Ordination.
3. Do you have to be chosen by God to speak His word or does the Holy Spirit play a role or both?

Thought to Remember

Some of you may or may not remember or even heard the old adage used by some that says "I know that I am preaching to the choir" or "you are preaching to the choir." Whenever this thought was expressed, the speakers were simple people who had the gumption to speak the truth, even if there may have been some indication that what they said might be repetitive. Everyone must have experienced a thorough talk from mom or dad, at one point in time. You knew when they were chewing you up one side and down the other – guess what? They were preaching. Is not that a good example of one of the definitions of "preaching"? If you know, believe and apply the Word of God, how can you make the distinction to the wrong doer or the lost in Christ, unless you speak the righteous truth in a loving manner?

Lesson 3: What Makes Us Go?

ROMANS 1:13-17
By Eugene Folks, Jr. and Sylvia Folks

Key Verse: So, as much as in me is, I am ready to preach the gospel to you that are at Rome also. (Romans 1:15)

After completing this lesson, the learner will be able to:

1. Tell others what motivates you to work in God's kingdom.
2. Analyze ministry work and its purpose.
3. Explain the Great Commission.

The only sure way for the "Great Commission" of Jesus to be fulfilled is based solely on the routine acts of God-loving, God-fearing, faithful, committed and believing Christian workers. Let us ponder for a moment the title "What Makes Us GO?" We can replace the word "makes" with other transitive verb replacements such as motivates, encourages, inspires, convicts, forces, reminds, causes, enables, etc...The key to the answer revolves around one's willingness and ability to go.

Paul boldly tells us in Scripture that the ideal situation for the people during his day and us today is to mimic him, in every way of the ministry. More often than not, whenever the church talks about New Testament Scripture one thinks about the influence of Paul because the consensus is to think highly of Paul and desire to serve like him. Any of us can be deemed willing and able, but that feeling serves no purpose unless passion plays a part. The word passion is a bit a strong, but that is intentional and exactly what is required to be persistent, consistent, faithful, adamant and dedicated to reach and achieve a desired goal or task. The expression of passion gives way to *love*, another strong word.

43

Our brother Paul had a passionate love for the Lord and all things related to the Lord. Where did he get this passion? He got it from the Lord. The conversion from the notorious Saul to the humbled Paul involved a change of thought. There was no loss of Saul's driven personality and stern character, during his conversion. In other words, God used what He had put in Saul, for His glory. The change of heart, mind and soul that came to Saul, while on the Damascus Road one day, consisted of only a few words from Jesus. Then suddenly, Saul became a changed man, with a new attitude. The one who had been diligent in persecuting Jesus was afforded the opportunity to hear from Jesus Himself. It was three days later that Saul was transformed into a new creature, by the indwelling of the Holy Spirit, with a renewed mission for the Lord (Acts 9). There is some speculation about Saul's name change to Paul, but the change continued to signify his divine change of heart. One thing is for sure; there is absolutely no way to have an encounter with Jesus and not leave changed. The main point of today's scripture reveals that Paul's ultimate objective was to get back to Rome, but there was so much work to do in the ministry that Paul could not resist.

Paul's story is touching and even motivating, but what is our personal story all about? The question is "What makes Us Go?" It would probably be more advantageous to talk about what makes us <u>not go</u>, but we do not want to promote any negativity that may cause us to keep making excuses. Let us encourage ourselves, in the work of the Lord. The Bible makes it clear that only what any of us do for Christ will last. There are a few attributes that will make us go anywhere there is a need and wherever the Lord is working. A fearless and confident attitude will be first among the attributes that causes us to go. A willing spirit to carry out the implied requirements in the commission will help us to go. The acknowledgment, love, and reverence for the Lord will motivate us to go. The intentional desire to care about the brothers and sisters in Christ makes us go. The reluctance of a selfish attitude will cause us to go. Understanding the individual as well as the church's purpose will help us to go. We all would do well to figure out and accept our purpose for ministry and identify the triggers that cause us to go or not.

Discussion Questions

1. Being honest with yourself first and foremost, what hinders you from staying the course and/or what makes you go wherever God is working?
2. Do you view ministry as something to do or work that needs to be done? Why? Why not?
3. Define what the elements of the "Great Commission" mean to you, in your own words.

Thought to Remember

The most important aspect of each of our lives is our spirituality into the truth, way, and life of Jesus. We are spiritual beings in a naturalistic, simple, complex and evil world. Our mission, as disciples of Christ, is to convert as many as possible to way of God and make them disciples who will make other disciples and continue to build a strong and mighty Kingdom for the Lord.

Lesson 4: God Commands us to Grow as Believers

PHILEMON 1:1-6
By Eugene Folks, Jr. and Sylvia Folks

> *Key Verse: That the communication of thy faith may become effectual by the acknowledging of every good thing which is in you in Christ Jesus (Philemon 1:6).*

After completing this lesson, the learner will be able to:

1. Examine why spiritual growth is a commandment.
2. Analyze proverbial statements within the context of the scripture and its setting.
3. Compare and contrast spiritual growth and development to natural child growth and development.

Whenever we talk about growth, in the natural sense of the word, we think of the human life span starting from infancy to adulthood. The saying that "age is only a number" is quite true, but the maturity level of a person is even more important. In God's mysterious way of taking care of us, He allows us a lifetime of "hard-knocks" and learning to reach maturity, in both the natural and spiritual realms. God wants each of us to grow in our love for Him, based on our belief, which is only as strong as our faith. The Bible says, *"now faith is the substance of things hoped for, the evidence of things not seen" (Hebrews 11:1).* This is one passage of Scripture that has a good church ring to it, but in reality it is a daunting challenge. It is almost impossible to reach spiritual maturity, without dealing with periodic faith-building circumstances. The title of this devotional message is fitting, because God's command for us to grow is crucial to our personal well-being, as well as equipping us to be ready and in position to give God glory, at various points in our lives. In other words, without growth, we cannot perform ministry to our highest potential of faithfulness. Without growth, we will become complacent, stagnant, and content with where we are and never desire to go further in the Lord.

In the text, Paul is writing to his co-laborer in the ministry, Philemon. Paul possessed a love for all who dedicated their life to the work and cause of ministry in Jesus Christ and Philemon was by far no exception. Paul was elated to commend Philemon for the love he had for the saints. There was no better complimentary blessing than intercessory prayer. Paul says that he is praying for Philemon, while encouraging him to keep the faith and continue the good work he started that will manifest itself in the faith building of others.

Brothers and sisters, you are encouraged to convey, spotlight, highlight, witness and share your experiences, history and belief in the Messiah, Jesus Christ. The Bible tells us, in no uncertain terms, that only what we do for Christ has meaning and will last a lifetime. Don't be so critical and judgmental of others. Have some compassion. The Bible tells us that the Lord is always looking for a few faithful saints to plant a seed of faith; water that seed and only God will bring forth growth in its due season. The more we discipline ourselves to obey and work as believing Christians, the more our belief in Jesus will grow, but growing in faith has never been prescribed as a choice, but it is a divine command.

Discussion Questions

1. Why is it necessary that God gives a command to grow, instead of making it optional?
2. There is an adage used by many that says "prayer changes things." How is that so?

3. The Bible says that faith equivalent to the size of a mustard seed is enough to speak to and move a mountain - why does that faith need to grow?

Thought to Remember

It is one thing to believe and have faith; but it is spiritual maturity that causes us to trust while waiting patiently.

UNIT 4: WISE SOUL WINNERS

Lesson 1: Soul Winning Evangelism

PROVERBS 11:30
By Christopher Walls, Sr. and Sheila D. Walls

Key Verse: The fruit of righteousness is a tree of life, and he who wins souls is wise (Proverbs 11:30).

After completing this lesson, the learner will be able to:

1. Define evangelism.
2. Explain how evangelism pertains to every believer in Christ.
3. Summarize why evangelism is important to the growth of the church.

Typically in today's society, you rarely hear Christians enthusiastically talk about evangelism. Yet, evangelism - or sharing the "good news" with those who do not know Jesus as their personal Savior - is what the Great Commission is all about. It is spreading the word! Every born again believer is charged with the awesome responsibility of winning souls for Jesus Christ by sharing the fact that He bled, died, and rose from the dead. Simple, isn't it?

The Word of God states in Proverbs 11:30 that *"he who wins souls is wise."* The fact that wisdom is needed indicates evangelism may not be as easy as it sounds. It appears that without wisdom, our attempts at evangelism can be ineffective and even counterproductive. The real struggle is in making the message relevant to the non-believer; to share the gospel in such a God-given way that it is meaningful and causes the love of Jesus Christ to shine forth.

How? The first thing to do is to pray for wisdom. Ask God to give you the wisdom needed to effectively win souls. It is important to simplify the gospel so that it makes sense to the nonbeliever.

Most people today do not talk in "King James" so you may need to speak in "plain" language. Know several scriptures and use them as references to support your witness. Share your personal testimony of how living for Christ has changed or impacted your life.

Identify and speak to their need. Even if they do not ask, most will want to know "what's in it for me?" Effective soul winning is personal as it touches the heart and gives hope! Jesus did not just die; He died for YOU! That means you do not have to die and go to hell. It also means you can live a victorious life here on earth.

While witnessing to others at church is important, the vast majority of evangelism happens outside of the church walls. Every interaction is an opportunity to share the good news! Many people needing to know the love of Jesus Christ will rarely, if ever, step foot into a local church. In John 20:21, Jesus tells His disciples "Peace to you! As the Father has sent Me, I also send you." GO! As a result of effective evangelism, souls will be won to the kingdom of God. Those who receive Christ become His disciples, and the cycle begins all over again.

Discussion Questions

1. Is evangelism still relevant? Why or why not?
2. How have you struggled to share the gospel of Jesus Christ?
3. How can you more effectively win souls to Christ?

Thought to Remember

Witnessing is just telling another person where to find spiritual nourishment.

Lesson 2: Evangelism is for Everyone

2 CORINTHIANS 5:14-21
By Christopher Walls, Sr. and Sheila D. Walls

> *Key Verse: Now then, we are ambassadors for Christ, as though God were pleading through us: we implore you on Christ's behalf, be reconciled to God (2 Corinthians 5:20).*

After completing this lesson, the learner will be able to:

1. Explain how evangelism pertains to every believer in Christ.
2. Discuss the perspective we have of other people, whether in Christ or not.
3. Define and explain reconciliation.

Typically God's expectation for His people, as it pertains to fulfilling His charge, always begins with us having a very firm internal belief (faith). This is what He has called us to do, as well as the way He has called us to do it is perfect. Evangelism, in itself, is a charge by Almighty God, to His people to see past the outward appearance and actions of the lost, and minister to their inner man (their spirit). This is the very thing Christ has done for us. He has looked past all of our imperfections and failings and engaged our spirit by His Spirit. This is where reconciliation takes place. Reconciliation allows us to be in right relationship with God because our sins have been imputed to Christ. Our slate is clean. We are forgiven. We now have the privilege of telling others that they can be reconciled to Him as well.

Being an ambassador for Christ, is the role of every born again believer. It is not for a select group of people who have been outfitted with special skills and experiences. While there are some believers who are called by God to commit their entire livelihood to evangelism, all of God's people will find this line item in their Christian job description. God fulfilled reconciliation through Jesus Christ. It is now His call to us for us to champion the cause of reconciliation with those we come in contact with. It is the banner we wave in all of our relationships, actions, and views. We are the conduit in the earth that God is using to bring reconciliation to those separated from Him.

While some would have you to believe that getting people to profess they believe in God is evangelism, the Word of God clearly states that true reconciliation is the goal. Verbally stating a belief in God is a stepping stone toward the ultimate goal, it does not fulfill the entire measure. God is calling us to continue our service with others until they have the true understanding that Jesus Christ died for their sins on Calvary's cross. For this reason, their sins are not imputed to them, as they should be (unto death). He loved us so much that He suffered death for people who have/had no knowledge of His sacrifice. This is the message we should carry, like flags at the forefront of a parade. This belief should blow in the winds of our lives while being anchored in our hearts.

Discussion Questions

1. How does God expect us to win other people?
2. What does it mean to be an ambassador for Christ?
3. Should reconciling others to Christ be the focal point for the modern day church?

Thought to Remember

A person that came to Jesus Christ as a result of evangelism should feel compelled to witness to others about Jesus.

Lesson 3: Jesus Is Calling You

MARK 3:7-19
By Terrence and Karen Kessee

Key Verse: And he ordained twelve, that they should be with him, and that he might send them forth to preach (Mark 3:14).

After completing this lesson, the learner will be able to:

1. Value the correlation between evangelism, the disciples, and himself/herself.
2. Identify the challenges he/she faces in presenting the gospel.
3. Discover the connection between the Philadelphia church and the church today in hindrances to evangelism.

Typically, most people find it an uncomfortable task when confronted with the evangelism of their faith. We have all or will at some point, be faced with evangelizing our faith. As well, Christ will most definitely ask us at the end of time if we met the challenges of this most indispensable task. This is the very task that He challenged all believers with in Matthew 28. When you accepted Jesus as Lord and Savior, you also were placed into the order of the Ecclesia. We are the Ecclesia, the ones who have been called out of this world and called into the fold of GOD.

Here is the exciting aspect of the call that Jesus has commissioned you with - we win! Now the most ominous apprehension is how we go about this task and how are we to be effective in this task. First, we must understand that we are not alone as Jesus has so graciously promised. His Spirit, our advocate, and counselor has endowed each of us as believers with a *dynamic* power. This is the power that is bestowed on all believers to achieve tasks through the utilization of the inherent abilities of Jesus Christ. Also, God will use others to bless us and keep us on the right course. We know the Bible speaks of iron sharpening iron (Proverbs 27:17) as a way for us to hold each accountable for our choices. Jesus did not need His disciples to complete His task of being our Savior, but most times He did not travel alone.

Let's examine the fact that Jesus did not evangelize alone. Inexplicably, Jesus took some of the most disdainful and questionable characters to partner with. The 12 disciples that Jesus chose are great examples for all of us as believers never to discount that we have a part to play in GOD's agenda for his Kingdom, no matter our background. Can you identify yourself in the 12? In the Old Testament, we are presented with Moses, who had a speech impediment, yet God used him and his ability as a catalyst for delivering the Israelites out of bondage. You were created for a purpose, and God has given you a unique characteristic for evangelism.

When we read and study Revelation 2, the church in itself is seen as having been challenged with so many obstacles. However, GOD did not hold back on His judgment of their actions. One of the most pointed observations of these passages was the fact that the church received explicit instructions on its purpose and the benefits given for those who listen to the call. Each passage ends with, "whoever has ears let them hear". Revelation 2 gives us reasons why it is so worth the risk of discomfort, ostracism, confrontation and other hindrances. One can have eternal life, no more death, and a place in God's divine hierarchy of government. Why would you hold back in spreading the gospel to a stranger? Why would you refuse to highlight the benefits of Kingdom Living to unbelievers? It is not only our responsibility but inexorably; it should be our passion.

Discussion Questions

1. Have you studied the lives of the 12 disciples, their personality, and their traits to identify with their ministry style? Find one whom you can identify with and examine how they used their character to write Scripture and how could you use your style to evangelize.
2. Have you prayed about the many excuses aimed at why you don't evangelize? Ask God for a boldness to share your faith with others.
3. What are the inherent abilities of Christ? How will you utilize these?
4. Study the persistency of the church of Philadelphia. Do you fit in this category of believers? If not, what are you going to do about it?

Thought to Remember

Jesus could have commissioned millions of angels to come and minister to the people of this earth; however, He created you. What greater way is there to express His love for us than to have others who love Him be an extension of His love to others?

Lesson 4: Witnessing In A Hostile World

JOHN 16:1-11
By Terrence and Karen Kessee

> *Key Verse: They shall put you out of the synagogues: yea, the time cometh, that whosoever killeth you will think that he doeth God service (John 16:2).*

After completing this lesson, the learner will be able to:

1. Develop a Biblical and studied response to persecution because of your faith.
2. Construct juxtaposition for evangelism.
3. Share the gospel in a hostile world.

The purpose for this lesson is to support those who evangelize and witness to others. Often, evangelism is not an easy task, and we are not loved or welcomed by those to whom we present the gospel. To be loved by others is a wonderful place to be; yet, there are times when this attribute is not so freely given by others. Our modern culture speaks to the aggressive nature as being the most accepted approach. Jesus knew about the ability of the Holy Spirit living within us as a precursor for counteracting these impulsive behaviors. This is where believers have to gravitate towards the wisdom and discernment from the Holy Spirit.

Being a voice for Christ in today's world has its pros and cons, or what seems to be cons. Evangelism is rewarding and challenging, but we must know that victory is an imminent promise from God. This passage in the book of John displays one of the final times Jesus is preparing His disciples with the many disappointments they may face after His departure. He desired to be as transparent as needed so that His disciples would not waiver from completing the Great Commission. Despite these projected mishaps, the disciples were gaining The Comforter to be in and around them as a sure guide and protector from the trials and tribulations this world had to offer them. As sentimentalists, we evoke the same compassion towards the ones we care about. Jesus knew the weaknesses of the flesh and sought to breathe strength into His disciples prior to the adverse encounters with a direct order to overcome the weight of the world.

We as believers have to understand that all harm is not intentional, and it could be stemmed from misunderstandings. Conversely, it can also be an all out onslaught attack on your faith. For a more definitive explanation, the enemy does not want you to witness for Jesus! Every major civilization in human history has abandoned God either in constant pressure to worship idol gods or the annihilation of those who evangelize about Christ. Even within the church body, we have experienced the harms of carnal deceptions and grief from the hands of other God-fearing believers. This can be one of the most misconceived encounters experienced in the church, especially for new or non-believers. This same concern was addressed in John 16:2. Persecution by those thinking their actions are inspired by God can lead to devastation and loss of faith. In America, being recipients of aggressive hostility for our beliefs is an unfortunate repeat of an egregious error.

Scripture gave us insight into the obstacles that we would have to encounter. Every interaction with a non-believer is an opportunity of advancing growth for God's Kingdom. However when opposition comes, we have to give attention to being Christ-like - meaning, blessing those who persecute you, loving on them with kindness, and never abandoning the call to action. To live is Christ, and to die (to self) is gain (Phil 1:21). This is the epitome of living for Christ and suffering for Him. Your reward is greater in the end.

Discussion Questions

1. What do you fear and why? Have you asked God to help you manage the emotional reflexes these trigger?
2. Have you ever considered constructing a juxtaposition for evangelism?
3. For those who have shown hostility towards you, are you persistently seeking God's direction for how to bless them?

Thought to Remember

Our victory comes from encounters, our encounters from opportunities, our opportunities come from submission and our submission comes from loving Christ!

UNIT 5: SHARING THE GOSPEL

Lesson 1: Great Expectations

LUKE 10:15-21
By Deborah Burch

Key Verse: In that hour Jesus rejoiced in spirit, and said, I thank thee, O Father, Lord of heaven and earth, that thou hast hid these things from the wise and prudent, and hast revealed them unto babes: even so, Father; for so it seemed good in thy sight (Luke 10:21).

After completing this lesson, the learner will be able to:

1. Distinguish the importance of spreading the gospel abroad.
2. Recognize that God has given us the power to overcome.
3. Identify God's proper placement for rejoicing.

Jesus, having all knowledge, saw fit to send the seventy out for the advancement of the Kingdom over 2,000 years ago. The world in which we live, both far and near, is filled with many people who are in need of salvation. Some are entangled in the sin of an environment that promotes hatred, idolatry, lust, lies and homosexuality. Many are bound by the deceitfulness of the enemy, being tossed to and fro. Most are trapped in society, having the ways of this wicked world, and not a mind to turn to Christ. But, all are in need of a Savior to set them free from the hand of the enemy. Through the preached Word and power of God, souls are set free. It behooves the born again believer to stand up and go abroad spreading the Gospel of Christ today just as in times past, that souls might be saved.

How good it is to know that God does not send the believer out unprepared. He gives them power (strength, energy, the ability to act effectively, with necessary means provided) that the task at hand might be doable. We notice that in the early days of the church, God gave His disciples power to overcome. They were given power to defeat or prevail over, to frustrate, to win, and conquer the enemy. We serve the same God, yesterday, today, and forevermore. Greater is He that is in the believer than he that is in the world. God has equipped the believer, making them more than conquerors through Christ Jesus.

The disciple/believer has much to rejoice in. Nevertheless, while it may seem befitting to gloat in the fact that one is being used of God, it is far better to highlight, focus upon, and rejoice in the fact that one has already been blessed by God. Just think, the very things believers promote (salvation, new life, and eternal glory) have already been bestowed upon them.

Discussion Questions

1. Is it important for the gospel to be spread abroad? If so, why?
2. In what areas has God given the believer power?
3. What should the believer base his joy upon?

Thought to Remember

Sharing the gospel is essential; but above all things, strive to ensure that your name is written in heaven!

Lesson 2: Not So Great Expectations

JOHN 15:18-27
By Deborah Burch

> *Key Verse: If the world hates you, ye know that it hated me before it hated you. If ye were of the world, the world would love his own: but because ye are not of the world, but I have chosen you out of the world, therefore, the world hateth you (John 15:18-19).*

After completing this lesson, the learner will be able to:

1. Identify with Christ as they partake of life in Him.
2. Recognize that when you know God, you have no excuse.
3. Understand that relating to and partnering with the Spirit of God is an imperative for every believer.

Today's lesson helps to put to rest the notion that when one is in Christ Jesus, he is exempt from the pressures of this world. As a matter of fact, we see through Scripture that not only will those in Christ experience worldly pressure, but in addition, every born again believer is also subject to ridicule, hatred, and persecution. As seen in our lesson text, when one identifies with Jesus Christ as Lord and Savior, they are automatically a target for the enemy. But Jesus does not leave the believer uncovered, ignorant, or without knowledge. Knowing that God is for you, more than the whole world against you and will never leave nor forsake you, the believer is expected to endure until the end.

Jesus expressed the formula of KNOW GOD = NO EXCUSE, and made it plain that those who have heard the truth with their ears and have seen his miraculous works with their eyes have no excuse for not believing. It is sin when we reject Christ, furthermore, to say we do not know Christ is to not know the Father and to deny Christ is to deny the Father. Likewise, Jesus identified the disciples with Himself that the believer would know that it is not so much about them, but more so about God and the God in them that is in question when one appears to be rejected. As believers, one should not take it personal when the God he represents is not received.

No one is capable of withstanding the wiles of the enemy on their own. Jesus sends the Comforter/Spirit of Truth that the people of God would be encouraged, strengthened, and taught what is necessary, that they might endure persecution. God is a very present help in the time of trouble and He will not leave His children comfortless. Every believer is empowered and expected to testify to the Glory of God, in season and out of season, in good times and in bad times, and whether they are received or not.

Discussion Questions

1. What are the strengths and limitations of being persecuted for Christ's name sake?
2. How does the knowledge and blessings of God make one accountable?
3. List and discuss some of the difficulties associated with being a witness.

Thought to Remember

In Christ, we experience not only mercy, but also malice, not only breakthroughs, but many breakups, and not only promises, but much persecution. Knowing this, remember that these light afflictions in which we now experience, are not worthy to be compared to the glory which shall be revealed!

Lesson 3: Intimidation on the Evangelism Field

NUMBERS 14:1-9; LUKE 9:13
By Deborah Burch

Key Verse: And all the children of Israel murmured against Moses and against Aaron: and the whole congregation said unto them, Would God that we had died in the land of Egypt! or would God we had died in this wilderness (Numbers 14:2).

After completing this lesson, the learner will be able to:

1. Discover that believers are called to have faith in God against all odds.
2. Tell that believers are commanded to trust in God.
3. Recognize that believers are charged to put their hope in God.

To believe is to have trust and faith, to accept as true, and to expect. In our lesson text, we are reminded that often times the people of God, if not careful, can find themselves having doubt concerning the word and promises of God. This doubt formed by fear can cause one to put their faith in ungodly places. Because God does not give us the spirit of fear, but of power and of love, and of a sound mind, the hand of the enemy and his spiritual weapons must be recognized, dealt with and put to rest. The Israelites found themselves so caught up in the issues of life and cares of this world that they were deceived into believing that they could be more comfortable in an uncomfortable place (Egypt), even if it meant bondage and forbearing the promises of God. It seems as though they had forgotten how to walk by spiritual faith, believing God for what they could not see, and were walking by their fleshly sight, placing focus and giving much attention to the enemy's distractions.

It is ungodly to bring into question (as if God is on trial) the leadership in which God has set up and put in place. Only ignorance, arrogance, and betrayal, wrought by the hand of the enemy can cause one to believe that his judgment is greater than that of God. The Israelites thought it good to defy God and make for themselves a captain of their own choice, one who would do as they said and seek after what they desired. Moses and Aaron thought it a shame before God and fell to their faces. Joshua and Caleb were filled with sorrow as they witnessed the lack of respect for and trust in God. The Israelites had come so far by faith, as they witnessed the hand of God in their lives, as He brought them out of bondage. Yet in their fear and distrust, they were unwilling to continue in the faith, that they might take possession of the Promised Land.

Throughout time, God has been tried and found to be true. He is not a man that He should lie. He is trustworthy and faithful to His every word. If God says it, it is so. Great is His faithfulness! He is faithful to see the believer through. Likewise, God requires faith on the part of the believer. For without faith, it is impossible to please Him. Knowing that with God all things are possible, it behooves the believer to hope in God Almighty, even when they find themselves facing impossible situations. If God can cause manna to fall from heaven, surely He can increase five loaves and two fish. Jesus commanded the disciples to follow His instruction to feed the people, not focusing upon their lack, but working with what they did have, while believing God to do the rest.

Discussion Questions

1. Why is having faith in God of great significance for the believer?

2. How are believers equipped to believe God for increase while facing lack?
3. What hinders the believer from believing the "All-Possible" God for the impossible?

Thought to Remember

God's hand of good is upon us, and His Word shall not return unto Him void; but shall accomplish all that He hath sent it out to do! If only we believe!

Lesson 4: Sharing the Gospel of the Resurrected Christ

LUKE 24:44-49
By Deborah Burch

Key Verse: And that repentance and remission of sins should be preached in his name among all nations, beginning at Jerusalem. And ye are witnesses of these things (Luke 24:47-48).

After completing this lesson, the learner will be able to:

1. Recall that without the death and burial, there would be no resurrection of Christ.
2. Recognize and remember the imperative to preach the Word of God to ensure believers are born again believers.
3. Explain that it is difficult to spread the gospel apart from being filled with God's Holy Spirit.

The Bible says that in all of one's getting, one ought to get an understanding. Even after the disciples walked with Jesus for a few years, the Lord still found it necessary to open up His disciples' understanding that they might have clear insight into all that He would speak unto them. How easy it is to confuse dedication with defeat. Jesus was dedicated to the cause pertaining the cross. It had been foreordained that Christ should suffer for the sake of man and that He should bear their punishment as payment for sin. If God Himself, manifest in the flesh having all power to override the excruciating pain He suffered and endured, thought it not fit to go against His own Word and law, how is it that man believes he will be able to somehow escape penalty for his work here on earth?

Jesus said that it is written and must be fulfilled. He died that all could obtain life through Him. God is a God of order and does not deflect from that which He has decreed. All too often we find those who highlight Jesus' resurrection without giving place to His death and burial or those who praise Him for His willingness to die and be buried for them without promoting that on the third day He rose with all power. The three, though separate entities, are held together as a threefold blessing. Jesus died and was buried so that He could rise and He rose because He died and was buried. Out of devotion, nothing and no one could stop Him from His death, burial, or grand resurrection.

Yes, all "receive power after that the Holy Ghost is come upon you; and ye shall be witnesses unto me", saith the Lord. In an ungodly world, filled with the wiles of the devil, principalities, powers, the rulers of the darkness of this world, and spiritual wickedness in high places, the Spirit of God is necessary. The disciples were instructed to wait in Jerusalem to be endued with power from on high before attempting to go forward, preaching in the name of Jesus. Preparation for ministry was then and is now of great importance as one faces an ever-challenging task of winning souls to Christ. God gives what is needed and believers must hold fast to the faith and rely on God for increase.

Discussion Questions

1. How does one effectively preach not only the death and burial, but also the resurrected Christ?
2. Is there any significance in preaching the name Jesus unto all nations? If so, explain.
3. Why is it important to wait for the indwelling power of God?

Thought to Remember

Whatsoever you do in word or deed, do all in the name of Jesus. For there is no other name given under heaven whereby men must be saved!

Lesson 5: Be Effective in Sharing the Gospel

JOHN 5:32-33; MATTHEW 11:7-11
By Deborah Burch

> *Key Verse: There is another that beareth witness of me; and I know that the witness which he witnesseth of me is true. Ye sent unto John, and he bare witness unto the truth (John 5:32-33).*

After completing this lesson, the learner will be able to:

1. Recall that being a witness does not require fame nor fortune.
2. Recognize that God's messengers are required to deliver God's message.
3. Discover that greatness is bestowed not earned, lest any man should boast.

In today's lesson, Jesus pointed out that anyone, regardless of their place in society or their financial status, could be called and used of God. John the Baptist, though not one of royalty in the world's system, was considered great in the Lord's eyes. Many who are called into ministry tend to put God's work on hold as they strive to be successful from the world's point of view. In this, some either never make it to God's call, due to an attempt to improve oneself first, or because after entering therein they realize that they never counted the cost and/or find themselves weak in the face of adversity.

John the Baptist is a great example of one focused upon the call of God over and above all else. With ministry comes sacrifice, and if one is able to press toward the mark of the high calling of God in Christ Jesus, his labor will not be in vain. Everything God calls for or does is with purpose and it is not His will that any should perish, but that all should have everlasting life. Knowing that the harvest is plentiful, but the laborers are few, the believer ought to be compelled to carry the message of Christ. John the Baptist was a true messenger sent by God and he was determined to speak the truth of God's word, as he purposed himself to deliver God's message and God's message only.

John the Baptist was the forerunner for Christ. He prepared the way for our Lord and Savior to come, and he was even privileged to baptize the Lamb of God which taketh away the sins of the world. How wonderful it is to know that with all John the Baptist accomplished in God, the least in the kingdom of God is considered greater than him. What a blessing of grace to be bestowed upon the people of God. Nothing in and of the believer, but because of our great and merciful God, we being counted as nothing in the world are deemed great in the eyes of God.

Discussion Questions

1. How does one speak the truth in a world filled with lies?
2. Are the men and women of God entitled to good fortune?
3. What is it that makes one great?

Thought to Remember

Belonging to the Kingdom of Heaven in and of itself is an honor. And because God is great, greatness is bestowed upon every born again believer!

UNIT 6: LOVING THE LOST

Lesson 1: Reaching the Lost

LUKE 10:1-9
By Niares A. Hunn

Key Verse: After these things the LORD appointed other seventy also, and sent them two and two before his face into every city and place, whither he himself would come He who hears you hears Me, he who rejects you rejects Me, and he who rejects Me rejects Him who sent Me (Luke 10:1).

After completing this lesson, the learner will be able to:

1. Identify the lost in need of salvation before the gospel is preached.
2. Recognize the importance of reaching and loving the lost.
3. Prepare evangelism teams to reach the lost.

The lost cannot be reached without love and without people. Notice when you received the Holy Ghost according to Acts 1:8, you were called to be witnesses to the lost, people who do not know Jesus Christ as their Lord and Savior. It takes people to reach other people. Once you are saved, you become a living epistle, known and read by men about the saving power of Jesus Christ. Thus, in our passage today, Jesus sends the disciples out two by two. He never sends them alone.

Jesus did not send them out alone, a strong indication that we all need the companionship of others. Even when we are witnessing or proclaiming the Gospel the Lord establishes this example because according to Luke 10:3, as God sends us on the Christian journey to witness to others we will be like lambs amongst wolves. Wolves run in packs and the saints of God need to work together in packs to destroy Satan's kingdom. Remember one can chase a thousand and two can chase ten thousand (Joshua 23:10; Deuteronomy 32:29-31).

Remember there is safety in numbers because a group has more protection than an individual. The Christian journey in itself can become challenging along with witnessing to those that are lost. Thus, it behooves us to travel in pairs so that one can pray, watch, and intercede while the other one shares the good news of the gospel: death, burial, and resurrection of Jesus Christ. Ecclesiastes 4:9-10 illustrates this point best by saying, "Two are better than one; because they have a good reward for their labour. For if they fall, the one will lift up his fellow: but woe to him that is alone when he falleth; for he hath not another to help him up."

The Lord never intended for us to travel alone on this Christian journey or to witness alone. We need friendship to witness while we serve and to support us as we transition in life. It is through this friendship or yoking together as a pair that we see God's love for us to remind us that He is our eternal friend and He will never leave us nor forsake us. It is this message that we should share with the lost, that if you want to have friends such as Jesus Christ, you must show yourself friendly because He is a friend that sticks closer than any brother (Proverbs 18:24).

Discussion Questions

1. Why is missionary work and evangelism so important?
2. Why do you think service or serving others is such an important principle in reaching the lost?
3. How do you feel when you see others in need of salvation? How do you decide when to help them?

Thought to Remember

The saints must redeem the time in order to reach the lost.

Lesson 2: Reclaiming the Lost

LUKE 15:1-10
By Jonathan W. Hunn, II

Key Verse: I say unto you, that likewise joy shall be in heaven over one sinner that repenteth, more than over ninety and nine just persons, which need no repentance (Luke 15:7).

After completing this lesson, the learner will be able to:

1. Explain why we should rejoice over a lost soul being reclaimed.
2. Express how we must see the lost through the eyes of Jesus Christ.
3. Recognize those things that hinder one from reaching out to the lost.

As I reflect on the new song, "Our Words Have Power" as rendered by the psalmist Lady Karen Clark-Sheard, I am realizing that we must always speak life into the dead situations in our life. Our son, daughter, or loved one may have strayed away from following the teachings of Jesus but rest assured - all is not lost. The dictionary defines *reclaim* as "getting back something that is lost or taken away". In the lesson today, Jesus proclaims that He has come to redeem us from the stain of sin. Once we are saved and redeemed we must share the gospel with others so that they are reclaimed from the hands of Satan.

In each of the parables written about the lost coin and the lost sheep that may have gotten lost due to the busyness of life; the sheep strayed from the sheep pin and the coin was misplaced by the owner. In either case, when something is lost or someone is lost and later reclaimed, we should rejoice that the person came back to God. The Lord wants us to come to Him in peace when He calls us to reconcile with the body of Christ. He desires to be in fellowship with all of His children so it is our duty as believers to help reclaim those who have gone astray.

Often times as I have read this passage, I am quite sure it has crossed the minds of others as well, "Why should one person matter out of thousands?" But Jesus does not look at it that way, He loves us each of equally and we are all important to Him. He does not pick favorites from his sheep in a flock. If one strays, then He will wait for that one to return. Thus, He wants us to act the same regarding our brothers and sisters. When God asks us to win souls and be accountable for our brethren our response should not be that of Cain's saying, "Am I my brother's keeper?" You are always held responsible for touching another's life in a positive manner.

Discussion Questions

1. Why is it our responsibility as believers to seek lost souls?
2. What things have you lost on your spiritual journey? What things do you need to consider losing to have a more effective relationship with God?
3. Who is responsible for us when we stray and become lost in our daily lives?

Thought to Remember

For the Son of man is come to seek and to save that which was lost. – Luke 19:10

Lesson 3: Leading the Lost with Your Light

LUKE 11:33-36
By Niares A. Hunn

Key Verse: No one after lighting a lamp puts it in a cellar or crypt or under a bushel measure, but on a lampstand, that those who are coming in may see the light (Luke 11:33 Amplified Version).

After completing this lesson, the learner will be able to:

1. Identify and name the lamp mentioned in the passage.
2. Distinguish between spiritual darkness and light.
3. Examine and recognize things that hinder the believer's light from bearing witness to Jesus Christ.

Have you ever found yourself in total darkness during a power outage? Well, if you have, you more than likely found it be quite challenging. Not necessarily in those familiar places such as navigating down the hall or to the bedroom, but rather through those unknown territories where it would be a lot easier to have sources of light. Well that is what the sinner is looking for from the believer, they know that life has its peaks and valleys, but they need someone to navigate them to the right path of stability until they have received Christ themselves and can learn to maneuver the Christian life.

Man has always been looking for new avenues to shed light into darkness and to preach the gospel in various ways to reach the lost. When the sinner can see the believer's light shining, it dispels fear and keeps them searching for someone that gives them better visibility to the things going on in their lives. People have heard that "Jesus is the light of the world" but if we are not bearing witness to the Light, it makes a difficult road to maneuver and get to Christ.

Thus, the Apostle Luke is admonishing believers to let the light of Jesus Christ shine brightly in your life. Don't hide your witness, light, or testimony that Jesus saved you for fear or by deeds of wickedness but instead allow Jesus to manifest Himself in your daily life and activities. You should live your life solely to please Jesus and to bear witness to the light. When you bear witness to the light, your life will be full of holiness, not sin. You will trim the wicker just like a coal oil lamp to keep the light of Jesus shining brightly in your life.

Discussion Questions

1. What does the lamp in Luke 11:33 represent?
2. Why is the lamp not hidden? Are you hiding your light? Why or why not?
3. Why does spiritual enlightenment depend upon the health of your spiritual eyes? What sharpens or dulls our spiritual discernment?

Thought to Remember

Let your light so shine before men, that they may see your good works, and glorify your Father which is in heaven. – Matthew 5:16

Lesson 4: The Lost that Reject the Gospel

LUKE 10:10-16
By Johnny and Doris Davis

Key Verse: He who hears you hears Me, he who rejects you rejects Me, and he who rejects Me rejects Him who sent Me (Luke 10:16).

After completing this lesson, the learner will be able to:

1. Identify the lost.
2. Recognize their fate.
3. Express the urgency of spreading the Good News.

People that hear the Gospel of Jesus Christ and reject its teaching are the lost. Ecclesiastes 1:2 best describes the life of the lost as one that is meaningless, useless, hollow, futile, and vain. Eternal separation from God is their final fate. Life is only worthwhile when it is based on God and His Word. The Gospel is the Good News, the salvation of the soul through Jesus Christ alone. The inhabitants of Capernaum, which was Jesus' headquarters while He was in Galilee, had many opportunities to hear His preaching and witness His many miracles. The people that rejected His teachings were held more accountable as unbelievers. Today Capernaum is deserted according to historical documents. Luke 10:16 tells us that "He who listens to you listens to Me; he who rejects you rejects Me; but he who rejects Me rejects Him who sent me." Rejecting Jesus is the same as rejecting God Himself.

The instructions given to the messengers of the Gospel to immediately leave any city that did not receive them was imperative because unbelievers destroy and disrupt fellowship and harmony that unites the believers of Christ. They were to wipe the dust of that city from them as a sign that the place was heathen and unclean. 2 Corinthians 6:14 says not to be unequally yoked together with unbelievers. Unbelief is destined to result in eternal destruction. We must heed the warning given to the unrepentant Gentile cities of Charozin and Bethsaida - Repent, the Kingdom of God is near. Jesus is coming soon.

Discussion Questions

1. Will judgment be the same for all unbelievers?
2. Why was Capernaum so harshly judged?
3. Why were the disciples told to leave any city that did not receive them?

Thought to Remember

The Lord is not willing that any should perish but that all should come to repentance (2 Peter 3:9).

UNIT 7: EVANGELISM THAT REACHES

Lesson 1: Early Church Evangelism

ACTS 5:12-16
By Latunya Farr

Key Verse: And believers were the more added to the Lord, multitudes both of men and women (Acts 5:14).

After completing this lesson, the learner will be able to:

1. Summarize how the early church was empowered by the Holy Spirit.
2. Explain the results of effective teaching.
3. Explore ways to reach others through sharing the gospel.

In this lesson, our focus will be on teaching. God empowers us to teach others about Him. After His resurrection, *Jesus came and spake unto them, saying, All power is given unto me in heaven and in earth. Go ye therefore, and **teach** all nations, baptizing them in the name of the Father, and of the Son, and of the Holy Ghost* (Matthew 28: 18-19). To "teach" means to be a disciple of one, to follow his precepts and instruction, to make a disciple, and to instruct. As the Body of Christ, God has empowered and commissioned us to teach the message of Jesus, through which He will draw all those who will believe unto Himself.

God empowers us to teach because it is the preaching of the gospel that reaches the heart of people. All our good intentions, innovations, and optimism even are at best watered down and ineffective if not balanced by the gospel of Jesus Christ. For it (the gospel) alone, is the power of God unto salvation to everyone that believeth (Romans 1:16). The apostles were ordered by the Jewish leaders not to teach in the name of Jesus. *And they called them, and commanded them not to speak at all nor teach in the name of Jesus*

(Acts 4:18). But it was the teaching and preaching of the gospel whereby lives were changed. Signs and wonders, miracles, unclean spirits cast out, and souls being added to the church come as a result of teaching and preaching the gospel.

It is never biblical to seek the results of the Word without teaching and preaching it first. The apostles put first things first; they were committed to preach and to teach all that they had seen, heard and experienced. Even when they were beaten and their lives threatened; they yet continued steadfastly in the gospel of Jesus Christ. *But Peter and John answered and said unto them, Whether it be right in the sight of God to hearken unto you more than unto God, judge ye. For we cannot but speak the things which we have seen and heard* (Acts 4: 19-20).

Discussion Questions

1. Discuss some of the signs and wonders experienced by the early church.
2. Does today's church experience fewer signs and wonders today? If yes, why do you think this is so?
3. What role did the Holy Spirit play in early church evangelism?

Thought to Remember

Miracles are still important today. They attract new believers, confirm the truth of the apostles' teaching, and demonstrate the power of a crucified and risen Messiah. Yes, miracles are still important in the church today!

Lesson 2: Individual Evangelism

ACTS 8:26-40
By Latunya Farr

Key Verse: Then Philip opened his mouth, and began at the same scripture, and preached unto him Jesus (Acts 8:35).

After completing this lesson, the learner will be able to:

1. Value Philip's obedience, dedication, and commitment to personal evangelism.
2. Identify any personal biases that hinder personal evangelism.
3. Implement a plan for personal evangelism.

I am a strong proponent of soul crusades, outreach teams, street revivals and other group events and activities that promote the saving of souls. They are needed, can be effective, and are often demonstrated in the Bible. However, let us not overlook the powerful impact of one-on-one, face-to-face, personal evangelism. Jesus ministered to great multitudes out in the desert, on mountain tops, and while sitting in a boat (Matthew 5-7; 9:35-37) - but He also ministered to people individually, such as Nicodemus (John 3:1-22), the Samaritan woman at the well (John 4:1-42), and Zacchaeus (Luke 19:1-10). Many times we draw back from personal witnessing because we are not a preacher or an evangelist. But the Bible says we have all been called to be a witness (Acts 1:8). Philip is a Biblical example of effective personal witnessing. *"He was not an apostle, he didn't have a famous name like Peter and Paul; but he was an effective and dedicated witness for Jesus"* (A Study in Personal Evangelism, Gene Taylor, pg. 20)[1].

Another hindrance to personal evangelism is that people feel like they don't know what to say or how to approach someone to share the message of Jesus Christ - but I like the example that Philip gives. Over and over it is said, "and being led by the Spirit", and "the Spirit said to Philip", and "the angel of the Lord spake unto Philip". It is essential to know the Word and to be able to teach the Word; however, to make it all work to the glory of God we must be led by the Spirit and not by a personal desire only.

God empowers us to teach. Evangelism that reaches is when we are able to start where the person is. God had already been working in the heart of this Ethiopian eunuch, now Philip would be used further, to water this soul unto water baptism. Philip was quick to obey and move according to the leading of the Spirit. Then he was patient enough to ask what the eunuch was reading and to access what he already knew. He prepared himself enough to be able to preach Jesus and after studying this lesson today we too should go and do likewise.

Discussion Questions

1. Discuss other Biblical examples when angels have been used to bring a message.
2. What is the importance of the Holy Spirit in ministering the gospel?
3. What are some hindrances to personal evangelism?

Thought to Remember

Keep your focus on saving souls and follow God's leading even if it seems like a demotion.

Notes

Taylor, Gene. (2005). *A Study in personal evangelism*. Retrieved from, http://www.ntslibrary.com/PDF%20Books/personal-evang.pdf

Lesson 3: Unplanned Evangelism

Acts 18:1-28
By Latunya Farr

Key Verse: Then spake the Lord to Paul in the night by a vision, Be not afraid, but speak, and hold not thy peace (Acts 18:9).

After completing this lesson, the learner will be able to:

1. Employ and remain steadfast even when the gospel of Christ is rejected.
2. Relate and learn to work in unity with others in the ministry of the gospel.
3. Recognize the importance of revisiting those who have been reached by the gospel.

In chapter 17 of Acts, Paul preached in Thessalonica and although some mocked and contended his teaching of Christ as the Messiah there were others who believed. As a result, Paul with the help of Silas and Timothy in Thessalonica established a church. But there was great contention and certain Jews, which believed not, opposed Paul and Silas desiring to kill them. Upon escaping with their lives, Paul and Silas travel to Berea and continued teaching and preaching Jesus in the synagogue of the Jews. Many believed on the Lord Jesus in the city of Berea, yet being pursued by Jews from Thessalonica, Paul is ushered to Athens.

While waiting for Silas and Timothy to meet him there, Paul is deeply stirred in his spirit by how the city is wholly given to idolatry. Paul preached unto them Jesus and the resurrection, and it was for the teaching and preaching of Jesus that Paul was brought to the council of Areopaguson Mars' Hill, which was the highest court in Athens. Certain philosophers of the Epicureans, and of the Stoicks, encountered him and demanded to know what these things meant. When they heard of the resurrection of the dead, some mocked: and others said, we will hear again of this matter. There were however small results in Athens.

After our study of evangelism in the early church and Paul's example of unplanned personal evangelism, we can now begin to shape our view of evangelism as part of our daily walk. All our evangelism efforts will not be individual witnessing or planned crusades. Therefore, we must be reliant on God at all times because we will have unplanned evangelism encounters, and unplanned situations, knowing that those people who cross our paths and circumstances that we encounter are all a part of God's perfect plan to brings souls into the kingdom of God.

Discussion Questions

1. Discuss how you would handle an unplanned evangelistic opportunity (Ex. at a grocery store, waiting room at the hospital, dentist, shopping mall, airline passenger turbulence, etc.).
2. How have you coordinated ministry efforts with others?
3. How do you handle ministry results, positive and negative?

Thought to Remember

Not everyone will be receptive to the gospel message but we must keep preaching and teaching it because the harvest is vast. And everyone will not refuse the truth of gospel - there are yet those who will believe and be saved.

Lesson 4: Compelling Evangelism

ACTS 9:1-22
By Latunya Farr

Key Verse: And he trembling and astonished said, Lord, what wilt thou have me to do? And the Lord said unto him, Arise, and go into the city, and it shall be told thee what thou must do (Acts 9:6).

After completing this lesson, the learner will be able to:

1. Observe how even the stoniest of hearts can be compelled by the gospel.
2. Examine and dispel feelings of fear and caution in witnessing to certain people.
3. Trust God to lead and instruct you as you minister in His name.

In our lesson today, the chief persecutor of Christians will become one of the greatest proponents of Jesus Christ. Saul of Tarsus was enslaved with zeal to destroy Christians. To him, they were enemy number one barring none. Saul destroyed their goods, imprisoned them, and threatened to imprison anyone who confessed Christ as their Savior - until the day the resurrected Jesus, Jehovah God himself, accosted and arrested Paul as he journeyed on the road toward Damascus. There shined round about him a light from heaven and Saul heard a most compelling gospel. "Who art thou Lord?", he asked. And to his astonishment, he hears the response: _I am Jesus whom thou persecutest: it is hard for thee to kick against the pricks._ What a shocker! In his zeal for God, he had been fighting against God himself.

The gospel that we teach and preach today is a compelling gospel. It's persuasive, gripping, captivating and it brings forth fruit. The gospel, the truth, the unadulterated Word of God is not weak or watered down. No! Just the opposite is true; it is powerful and brings forth results. Saul heard the compelling gospel from Jesus Himself. And the result of hearing the words of Jesus, was that Saul was broken and contrite in spirit. Saul was awakened to his sinful state and he was three days without sight, and neither did eat or drink. And he struggled and questioned who could deliver him from the law of sin and death. But Ananias being obedient to God despite his own personal feelings went to Paul and ministered unto him. Paul found that the God that had arrested him on the road to Damascus was the same God who could deliver him.

*...Brother Saul, the Lord, even Jesus, that appeared unto thee in the way as thou camest, hath sent me, that thou mightiest receive thy sight, and be filled with the Holy Ghost. And immediately there fell from his eyes as it had been scales: and he received sight forthwith, and arose, and was baptized (*Acts 9:17-18).

Discussion Questions

1. Why did Paul have such a strong hatred for Christians?
2. What was Paul's response to the truth revealed by Jesus on the road to Damascus?
3. Ananias' original response to God that Saul would become a Christian was, "Not him Lord, that's impossible. He could never become a Christian!" What person(s) do you have the same feelings regarding their probability of being saved?

Thought to Remember

Sometimes God breaks into a life in a spectacular manner, and sometimes conversion is a quiet experience.

UNIT 8: EVANGELISM THAT REACHES AND REVIVES

Lesson 1: Sowing Seeds

LUKE 8:4-13
By Niares A. Hunn

> *Key Verse: Now the parable is this: The seed is the word of God (Luke 8:11).*

After completing this lesson, the learner will be able to:

1. Maximize the seed of the Word of God that promotes one's own faith and provokes one to share the gospel.
2. Examine the types of soil in the evangelism field.
3. Develop relationships that produce fertile soil.

As we travel along this Christian journey, the thought may run through our minds, is there more to this life? The answer is an emphatic, yes! But we must do business and occupy until He comes (Luke 19:13). We must be about the Father's business (Luke 2:49) going into the hedges and highways compelling men and women to come to Christ (Luke 14:23). All throughout the gospel of Luke, the focus was on Jesus fulfilling the role of the suffering servant as Isaiah prophesied in Isaiah 52:13-53:12.

He realized that Jesus was fulfilling this role by giving His life as a ransom for many and by humbling Himself in the form of a servant. Everywhere that Jesus went He served them spiritual food and natural food. However, the spiritual is not first, but the natural; then the spiritual according to 1 Corinthians 15:56 (New American Standard Bible). He always ministered to the total person. Likewise, as we minister to those we encounter in our day-to-day lives, we should be prepared to minister to them in every aspect of their lives, those things that they need naturally and spiritually. This

97

will ensure that the seed of the Word of God is productive and able to bring forth a harvest.

As we share the Word of God with others, we must do our best to make sure that the seed of the Word of God does not fall by the wayside and become rejected by those to whom we share the gospel. We know that offenses will come because of the Word of God but we want to be sure that we give the Word of God a chance to germinate in their hearts to make sure that they fully understand what we are sharing with them, the opportunity to live with Jesus in heaven.

In our sharing about the ultimate prize of heaven, we must stress the importance of continuing in the faith and obedience to the Word of God. We don't want those with whom we sow seeds of the gospel to think that they respond to the Word of God and then allow it to fall upon stony ground and not be watered, developed, and groomed. They must realize their response is a lifetime commitment to follow Jesus.

This commitment requires them to follow up by devoting their time, talent, and treasure to the Kingdom of God. Again we don't want them excited about following Jesus and allow the Word of God to fall among thorns and allow the cares, riches, and pleasures of this life to pull them back into the world. As the sower of the seed, again you must minister to the needs of the whole person so that they can bear fruit that matures into perfection. We want the Word of God to fall on good ground, which springs up and bears fruit by responding to the gospel in obedience and with a ready heart to receive all that God has for them.

However, success is never guaranteed when seeds are sown. We see this even in our passage today. Jesus sowed seeds and 1 out of 4 was productive but this did not prevent Him from sowing the seed. Twenty-five percent is not bad when we keep things in perspective, can you imagine having $25 out of $100 in this economy or better yet $25,000 out of $100,000 because little becomes much in the hands of God. We never know how the seed will germinate and take root because according to 1 Corinthians 3:6 it states that I have planted, Apollos watered; but God gave the increase. We are not privy to whether that one soul will become the next Billy Graham, Amy Wilson Carmichael, or Dr. Ben Carson. We must continue to sow the seed regardless of the outcome but it can only be maximized and developed from relationships that are: (1) rooted in love, (2) led by the Spirit of God, and (3) discerned based on the type of soil that the sower is sowing into. All ground is not good ground but regardless, we must sow the seed and leave the results to God.

Discussion Questions

1. What kind of heart are you offering to God?
2. As a believer, are you sowing and sharing the gospel seed?
3. Do you think that the terms of discipleship should be explained upfront or after an individual has been saved?

Thought to Remember

"They that sow in tears shall reap in joy. He that goeth forth and weepeth, bearing precious seed, shall doubtless come again with rejoicing, bringing his sheaves with him (Psalm 126:5-6).

Lesson 2: Returning For Revival

HOSEA 14:1-7
By Lorie Thornton

Key Verse: O' Israel, return unto the Lord thy God; for thou fallen by thine iniquity (Hosea 14:1).

After completing this lesson, the reader will be able to:

1. Comprehend the result of sin in the life of the believer.
2. Understand the importance of repentance.
3. Realize God's willingness to forgive and restore His people back to Himself.

The purpose of this lesson is to examine and understand the result of sin and the effects it has in the life of the believer. During this lesson, we will also discuss the plan that God has in place to restore His people to righteousness in the event of sin in their life.

Today we live in a world that has turned from biblical principles and commandments of the Lord. We have become consumed with the cares of the world and the world's system. We are now a world that has replaced the Word of God with degrees, positions, economic status and the world's system of doing things. While there is nothing wrong with getting a secondary education, a position, or wealth, the danger is when we esteem them higher than the will and commandments of God. When we place anything or person higher than God in our lives, we have now fallen into idol worship. God's Word should take precedence over everything in your life when you are baptized and a born again believer. Idolatry is sin and sin separates us from God. Sin in the life of the believer literally keeps the hand of God from operating fully in the life of the believer. Because we are in the dispensation of grace, the Lord will still have a measure of grace and mercy in the life of the believer if they have fallen into sin; but, this is not His desire. The Lord wants to fully restore us to Himself.

Just as the prophet Hosea came and exposed the sin of the Israelites, he also gave them the solution how to be restored back to right fellowship with the Lord. This is the same thing pastors are doing every service when they preach the Word of God, they are exposing the sinful lifestyles and disobedience as compared to God's Word, while at the same time offering the people the only solution to right their offenses against God. Despite the sinful ways of the people, God says in His Word, if we repent and turn from sin He will forgive because the blood of Jesus has been applied to our lives. Through the power of the Holy Ghost we will be restored, renewed and revived because of our obedience to God's only plan of forgiveness which is repentance and turning from our ungodly ways and turning to the Lord. The Lord has promised He is faithful and just to forgive our sins and free us from all unrighteousness (1 John1:9). His anger and wrath will be no more and He will restore prosperity to us and our land (2 Chronicles 7:14). Because of the love the Lord has for His creation and His children, He will forgive us when will follow the plan He has laid out in His word, which is repentance. The will of the Lord is that no man should perish. He redeemed mankind to Himself when He died on the cross at Calvary and rose from the grave. He also gave His children the ability to be restored to Him when they turn away from sin, through repentance. The Lord promised to restore and revive His children, He promised to heal the land and prosper His people. When restoration comes by way of repentance, it results in complete access and fellowship with the Lord.

Discussion Questions

1. Is it possible to sin without knowing and if so, is repentance required?

2. Name three ways to keep yourself in obedience to the will of God.
3. What is the key component in God's ability to forgive us of sin?

Thought to Remember

The love of God has made provision for every fallible part of our life. Acknowledgment, Confessing, and Turning equals total restoration in God.

Lesson 3: Bridge Builders

JOHN 4:1-30
By Sharonda N. Littleton

Key Verse: Jesus answered and said unto her; whosoever drinketh of his water shall thirst again: But whosoever drinketh of the water that I shall give him shall never thirst; but the water that I shall give him shall be in him a well of water springing up into everlasting life (John 4:13-14).

After completing this lesson, the learner will be able to:

1. Express the importance of evangelizing.
2. Recognize that evangelizing is love.
3. Demonstrate that evangelizing is more than a title, but a call.

Evangelizing is a key fundamental that every Christian should equip themselves in. *Romans 1:16-17 (NASB) declares; for I am not ashamed of the gospel, for it is the power of God for salvation to everyone who believes, to the Jew first and also to the Greek. For in it the righteousness of God is revealed from faith to faith; as it is written, "BUT THE RIGHTEOUS man SHALL LIVE BY FAITH."* There are 57 bible verses that encourage every believer to be a living vessel for this gospel, and to be believers that proclaim the message that Jesus exclaimed to so many!

The woman at the well was one of many that needed spiritual deliverance from her sin, although in her mind, she felt as though she was doing what was necessary to survive. According to biblical studies, a woman during that time often had very limited options for survival; to marry, become a beggar, or a prostitute, and the woman at the well chose the latter of the three for she knew that the man she currently laid with was not legally her husband. She also knew of her many sins! She was shunned by others in Samaria because of her lifestyle.

Jesus knew of her condition. He knew she needed to turn from her sinful lifestyle. He also knew what she could become by having newness of life. Never once did Jesus make her feel less than human, but yet He began to tell her about the living water that she could obtain in order to become a candidate for eternal life. Jesus showed her love and compassion even though it was customary to forsake any Samaritan due them being mixed race Jews, Jesus yet showed her love.

Showing respect and love is essential while evangelizing, especially when we know individuals on a personal level, we must be blinded by what they do so that they can freely become who they need to be by hearing the "Good News"! Jesus wants all to know of the living water that is only obtained through Him. Evangelizing allows for one to give up "self "for the purpose of ministry. Humility is also an important virtue to have while working to build the kingdom. One may ask why humility? Well, humility allows you to see others as God sees them! You're able to look beyond an individual's frailties and faults so that you're able to love them as Christ has commanded us to love. That then opens the door for evangelistic ministry to take place.

Discussion Questions

1. How did Jesus' one act of kindness to a sinner build a bridge to evangelize her?
2. Was Jesus wrong for pointing out her sin before giving her the gospel?
3. Is this an effective way to evangelize? Is this the only way to evangelize? Are there other methods?

Thought to Remember

God commands us to love each other; for, without love being exhibited one to another there is no hope for us to draw individuals that are broken-hearted and downtrodden to the Kingdom of God!

Lesson 4: Family Evangelism

ACTS 10:36-48; ACTS 18
By Niares A. Hunn

Key Verse: When I call to remembrance the unfeigned faith that is in thee, which dwelt first in thy grandmother Lois, and thy mother Eunice; and I am persuaded that in thee also (2 Timothy 1:5).

After completing this lesson, the learner will be able to:

1. Organize and balance their home, ministry, and work obligations.
2. Appraise family evangelism and kingdom building.
3. Describe the results of family evangelism when the gospel is preached.

Today's lesson will focus on the two-fold aspects of family evangelism, meaning a family that serves in the ministry together and a family that becomes followers of Christ together. This lesson is very powerful because it focuses on several things that should catch your attention about Acts 18 and how it is applicable today. Aquila and Priscilla are an example of a godly couple that serves the Lord together with Paul on missionary journeys (evangelism) as well as having a house church (ministry) where they pastor and shepherd believers.

This story is so crucial in an era where often times unless a woman is the full-time shepherd she is often overlooked by the parishioners due to the esteem given to her husband. But in the scriptures that we read in the New Testament where they are mentioned together at least 6 times, (Acts 18:2; Acts 18:19; Acts 18: 24-28; Romans 16:3-5; 1 Cor. 16:19; 2 Timothy 4:19) her name often appears first probably due to her being the most active in the church. It is from these six passages where they are mentioned that we see that they were in Rome, Italy (Romans 16:3-4); Corinth (Acts 18:2-18); Ephesus (Acts 18:19; 24-28; 1 Corinthians 16:19; 2 Timothy 4:19), and traveled with Paul extensively to spread the gospel of Jesus Christ. This places a value on how God can use a godly couple in the kingdom to (1) establish churches, (2) shepherd God's people, and (3) proclaim the gospel of Jesus Christ.

It is the proclamation of the gospel that brought salvation to the house of Timothy, his grandmother Lois, and his mother Eunice as the Apostle Paul traveled to preach the gospel to Gentiles and Jews. Likewise, the Apostle Peter also traveled extensively to share the gospel with mainly Jews and in Acts 10:36-48 with a Gentile family as well. It is this proclamation that allows the gospel to penetrate the hearts of the entire family that all of them were converted. But even after conversion, family evangelism, whether working in the ministry or just recently being converted, can be strenuous for a family. All may be converted, but all may not serve in the same capacity or with the same degree of passion.

Thus, it is vital that balance is maintained between work, family, and ministry obligations. This can be achieved by (1) charting a weekly schedule, (2) scheduling time for a date night or family night for an outing or event that can be done as a couple and/or done as a family with the children, and (3) schedule a quarterly serving time together perhaps at Thanksgiving to feed the homeless at a shelter. Finally, the most important thing about family evangelism is scheduling a weekly time to pray, fast, and read God's Word together as you serve in God's kingdom.

Discussion Questions

1. Describe the ministry of Aquila and Priscilla.
2. What were the results of Paul's preaching?

3. How would your spouse or children evaluate you as a spouse or parent? What would they say?

Thought to Remember

A family that prays together stays together.

UNIT 9: PREPARING FOR EVANGELISM

Lesson 1: Equipping the Saints Part 1

EPHESIANS 4:11-16
By Savannah G. Jones

Key Verse: Which is the head, even Christ: from whom the whole body fitly joined together and compacted by that which every joint supplieth, according to the effectual working in the measure of every part, maketh increase of the body unto the edifying of itself in love (Ephesians 4:15b-16).

After studying the lesson, students should be able to:

1. Recognize why God gave leadership in the church.
2. Explain how the saints are equipped before witnessing.
3. Communicate why unity is essential.

Ephesians is one of four letters written by Paul in prison. It was a letter circulated to the churches in the provinces of Asia. Paul's letter to the Ephesians did not address any particular problem as he did to the Corinthian church concerning their moral and spiritual state (1 Corinthians 1:10-13). However, there was division among the people as to whom they should follow - Paul, Apollos, Cephas or Christ. Paul's answer to them was that there should be unity in the church and that Christ is the only one who died and gave Himself for their salvation. God called them into fellowship with his Son, our Lord Jesus Christ. God did not give leadership in the church to bring division, but to unify the saints that they might be equipped for evangelism.

I. THE LEADERSHIP IN THE CHURCH

¨And he gave some, apostles; and some, prophets; and some evangelists; and, some, pastors and teachers; For the perfecting of the saints, for the work of the ministry, for the edifying of the body of Christ¨ (Ephesians 4:11-12). God gave gifted men to the Church, the twelve apostles who were chosen by Jesus Himself who also gave the Great Commission in Matthew 28:19. He gave prophets, not foretelling the future, but who expounded on the Word of God. He gave evangelists and missionaries traveling both within the homeland and on foreign soil, that helped the church to grow by augmentation. Pastors and teachers are individuals, who in God's plan are able to instruct and feed the saints by expounding on the rich Word of God unto the saints. Each office works together, equipping the saints for the building of the Body of Christ.

II. THE EQUIPPING OF THE SAINTS

According to Webster's Dictionary *equip, equipped*, or *equipping* means making ready to provide with what is needed or to prepare by training or instruction. You may choose either one of these words and definitions, but whichever you decide to select, it is important to know that God has equipped the leaders with everything they need to feed God's people. According to Ephesians 1:17-19, God has given you all the power to use by the renewing of your mind and since your mind is being renewed by the Word of God; then what is the exceeding greatness of his power to us-ward who believe, according to the working of his mighty power. It is God's power who works in the life of the leaders to preach and teach the gospel to others in their communities and abroad. Every child of God should desire to have an experience with God and should desire that the holiness of God is displayed in their lives. They should also desire to be set apart for God so that He can use them in any area of ministry. According to 2 Corinthians 7:1 every person must cleanse themselves from all filthiness of the flesh and the spirit not just leaders: evangelists, pastors, or teachers. Every believer should desire to be holy. Yes, evangelists, pastors and teachers are to prepare the saints for the building of the Body of Christ, by sending them out with a desire to bring the lost sinners to Christ but the saints have to do their part as well by having the desire to serve God and the desire to be sanctified and set apart for the Master's use.

III. THE UNITY OF FAITH

Jude's exhortation to every Christian was to "earnestly contend for the faith which was once delivered unto the saints." This is not a one-time act, we must earnestly contend for the faith according to Ephesians 4:13 - *Till we all come in the unity of the faith, and of the knowledge of the Son of God, unto a perfect man, unto the measure of the stature of the fullness of Christ.* Unity of faith is walking, talking, and striving for the perfection that is apprehended in Christ as found in the Word of God in Philippians 3:12-13 and Luke 9:62. The church is to resemble Christ in every way. Therefore, every wind of doctrine will not move the mature saint, but it will for those who are spiritually immature (1 Corinthians 3:1). Paul is saying you are yet carnal as babes in Christ if you do not know the scriptures, nor study, seeking for the understanding of the word of God. Today there are many different doctrines - if you are not rooted and grounded in the word of God, you will be deceived.

IV. THE WHOLE BODY

God made the human head and human body an illustration of the relationship between Jesus (as the Head of His Body) and the Church (each saint being a member of that body). Christ as the Head is the source of growth but we must study, pray, and read His Word so that we can mature and grow. As we study we are able to help others to mature and grow in Christ as we share what God has given to us. This is why God equipped the church with evangelists, pastors, and teachers in Christ to help us mature and grow as a body of believers.

Discussion Questions

1. Do all saints have faith?
2. How does this lesson challenge you? Discuss.
3. What does "speaking the truth in love" mean?

Thought to Remember

Jesus' prayer in the Garden of Gethsemane before His betrayal, is for unity of His disciples. Just as Jesus and his Father are unified, Jesus prays that His disciples be one as well (John 17:21-23).

Lesson 2: Equipping the Saints Part 2

LUKE 16:19-31
By Tammy N. Jones

Key Verse: For I have five brethren; that he may testify unto them, lest they also come into this place of torment (Luke 16:28).

After studying the lesson, students should be able to:

1. Explain why the rich man went to hell.
2. Connect sin, repentance, and salvation with Abraham's bosom.
3. Express the importance of repentance and evangelism in our culture today.

The Gospel of Luke is one of two books written by Luke. It is the third book of the Gospels and the second longest of the four. Luke the Physician was converted in Antioch. His writing of the book of Luke and Acts help us understand the life of Jesus Christ while here on earth and our need for salvation.

Our lesson picks up in Luke 16:19-31. This parable is told by Jesus concerning a rich man and a man named Lazarus. The rich man in his fine purple linen, enjoyed the finer things of life. Meanwhile, Lazarus lay at the gate of his home hoping to get a crumb from his table while dogs licked his sores. The rich man and Lazarus died but ended up in two different places.

I. The Sin and Repentance

The rich man did not go to hell because of his money. The lack of salvation and a relationship with God brought about his damnation. In verse 19 it tells us how the rich man enjoyed the finer things in life, but never once mentioned him having a relationship with God. The Bible lets us know that "the wages of sin is death; but the gift of God is eternal life through Jesus Christ our Lord" (Romans 6:23).

As a sinner, there must be repentance. You may ask, what is true repentance? Repentance is to leave the sin that we have loved before and show that we are grieved by it by doing it no more and turning to the Lord. "For godly sorrow worketh repentance to salvation not to be repented of: but the sorrow of the world worketh death" (II Corinthians 7: 10). There must be godly sorrow in order for repentance to come. The rich man realized much too late that he needed to repent. For that reason, he lifted up his eyes in hell.

II. Salvation & Evangelism

In our key verse (v.28), the unnamed rich man asks father Abraham to send Lazarus to his father's house to tell his five brothers about salvation because he did not want them to join him in torment. Abraham reminded him that they must hear Moses and the prophets. If they do not listen to the living saints proclaiming the gospel neither will they listen to a saint that has died and come back from the dead to preach the gospel.

Therefore, today the saints must be the voice that cries in this dying world, "REPENT". Matthew 9:37b, lets us know that "The harvest truly is plenteous, but the labourers are few". Unless we as a people, (the body of Christ), spread the gospel among our friends, family, and everyone we meet, they will not be able to hear the message of salvation. Hell is REAL and is not a joking matter. We must get to work; "I must work the works of him that sent me, while it is day: the night cometh, when no man can work" (John 9:4).

Discussion Questions

1. Why must there be repentance of sin?
2. What is the importance of evangelism?
3. Have you witnessed to your friends and family?

Thought to Remember

Lazarus was not saved because he was a poor man or sickly. Sins are not forgiven in that way. Jesus' blood alone cleanses us from all unrighteousness. Jesus Christ is our only hope of salvation and we must hold fast to Him or be lost.

Lesson 2: Faith and Evangelism Part 1

ISAIAH 9:2-7; TITUS 2:11-14
By Savannah G. Jones

> *Key Verse: The people that walked in darkness have seen a great light: they that dwell in the land of the shadow of death, upon them hath the light shined (Isaiah 9:2).*

After studying this lesson, students will be able to:

1. Explain the sacrifices of the believer to evangelize people walking in darkness.
2. Be empowered by God to share their faith through evangelism.
3. Discuss the believer's exercising of their faith to evangelize.

Isaiah has 66 chapters, the first 39 chapters corresponding with the Old Testament and the last 27 corresponding with the New Testament. In reading the prophetic scriptures that Isaiah has written, one can clearly see that the Lord is the God of Israel and the chosen people whom the Messiah will come through. They therefore, stand in a peculiar relationship to God. In Isaiah 11:1, we read of Jesus' human descent and what characteristics He will possess. They are also further explained in Isaiah 9:6 "For unto us a child is born, unto us a son is given". We find:

1. Government upon His shoulder
2. His name will be called Wonderful Counselor
3. Mighty God
4. The everlasting Father
5. The Prince of Peace

(Isaiah 7:14; Luke 2:11; John 3:16)

It is these prophecies about Jesus that encourages and builds our faith. These facts and prophecies as written in the scripture confirm one another and they confirm that Jesus is the Savior of the world just like the Word of God has declared. Just as Jesus served humanity by sacrificing His life so that we can share the salvation story, God also requires men and women today to sacrifice their time, talent, and treasure to evangelize and spread the gospel. Remember the gospel message is what Isaiah prophesied would come and it is yet going forth today!

I. God Empowers Men for Service

God empowers men to serve by giving them the Holy Ghost but it is the grace of God that brings salvation (Titus 2:13-14). Just as the disciples were filled with the Holy Ghost on the day of Pentecost, Peter was given the power to witness and three thousand souls were added that day. The disciples were bold in their witnessing just as Philip was in Samaria with the Eunuch (8:5-39). Thus, teaching sound doctrine is essential for preachers, they should guard against laying a wrong foundation. We must preach that salvation is free but Jesus paid for our sins with His life. Hence, we should want to deny ourselves of worldly and sensual pleasures to live for Him and to be a godly witness.

II. Faith and Evangelism

The calling of God is essential in evangelism - not just for ministers only, for Jesus told the disciples to go to Jerusalem and wait for the Holy Ghost (Acts 1:8). Every man, woman, boy and girl is required to win souls for Christ. When you make a cake, if it is delicious you will tell everybody to taste it (Psalm 34:8). The devil wants the people of God to be afraid to witness on their jobs, at school, while shopping, and anywhere that we go. The world is looking for hope from the government, the police officers and laws are unfair, there is depression and stressful situations, and people do not know where to turn (Romans 10:17). Isaiah 9:2 tells us that "The people that walked in darkness have seen a great light: they that dwell in the land of the shadow of death, upon them hath the light shined".

Discussion Question

1. What part of the lesson challenged your life?
2. Discuss the condition of the world and how it relates to Isaiah.
3. Discuss the two ways in which God imparts His grace.

Thought to Remember

The greatest gift given to man is Jesus dying on the cross to give man life.

Lesson 4: Faith and Evangelism Part 2

JOHN 1:1-18; PSALM 96
By Savannah G. Jones

Key Verse: The same came for a witness, to bear witness of the Light, that all men through him might believe (John 1:7).

After participating in this lesson, each learner will be able to:

1. Explain why mankind needs Jesus.
2. Describe why Jesus is referred to as the "True Light".
3. Share God's love for man.

Apostle John is the writer of the Gospel of John, although he does not mention himself as the writer. John and his brother James were the sons of Zebedee and Salome, and they were chosen by Jesus to be His disciples. John's place of birth was Bethsaida of Galilee and he was a fisherman by trade. John is known for his close relationship with Jesus, he was known as "the disciple whom Jesus loved" and "the beloved disciple." You can learn that love is the "heart of Christ" as you read the messages John.

In the book of Psalms, we learn about the awesomeness of God. David tells us to make a joyful noise when we come in the presence of God. His praise of dancing before the ark was witnessing to the people the King of Israel that his royalty would not hinder his praise. He came out of his royal robe to praise his God, which made his wife angry with him; but he let her know that she had not seen anything yet when it came to praising his Lord and Savior. David should have died, when he committed adultery with Bathsheba, instead God's grace have him life.

Likewise, if our lifestyle bears witness to our deliverance from sin, then, you will also give God praise in the dance. Ever since the beginning of creation, we were made to praise and glorify God. Our life should be a testimony of God's saving power.

I. The Life of Man

There have been different views on the study of creation. This lesson will not attempt to provide answers, but will attempt to examine the biblical record of creation. The Bible begins with the words, "In the beginning God created" (Genesis 1:1). Also, the Gospel of John begins with the words, "In the beginning was the word and the Word was with God, and the Word was God" (John 1:1). John is saying that the Old Testament and the New Testament reveal and testify about who Jesus is.

Man was created in the beginning from the dust of the ground and when God breathed into him life, man became a living soul. But after man sinned, he needed God to give him life again, because his life was no longer full of light – he now dwelt in spiritual darkness.

II. The True Light

John was sent before Jesus to lead people out of darkness by telling them that Jesus was coming as the true light of the world and to baptize them with the Holy Ghost. When Jesus began His preaching He was rejected by the elders and chief priests because they disapproved of Jesus' ministry (Matthew 21:42; Mark 8:31; 1 Peter 2:4,7). Jesus is the light of the world (2 Corinthians 4:6; Ephesians 5:14; John 12:44-50) and Paul and Barnabas were commanded to be light to the Gentiles as well (Acts 13:47). As believers, we are to witness that Jesus is light of the world (1 Peter 2:9; Psalm 96:1-8) through our lifestyle which testifies about our faith in Jesus Christ.

III. Jesus' Love for Mankind

John had an intimate love for Jesus, he was close enough to Jesus, that he was called the "beloved disciple". The child of God must have that intimate love with God. In the gospel of John you see Jesus showing love and compassion for the people. *"For we have not an high priest which cannot be touched with the feeling of our infirmities; but was in all points tempted like as we are, yet without sin. Let us therefore come boldly unto the throne of grace, that we may obtain mercy, and find grace to help in time of need"* (Hebrews 4:15).

Discussion Questions

1. Discuss what you received out of the lesson.
2. How can you be a witness of the True Light?
3. Discuss why some people reject sinners for what they are doing instead of witnessing to them.

Thought to Remember

In order to witness, you must understand that souls *need* the True Light - Jesus.

UNIT 10: TOOLS FOR THOSE THAT DISCIPLE

Lesson 1: Prayer before Discipleship

COLOSSIANS 4:1-6
By Paul H. Evans, Sr. and Helen R. Evans

Key Verse: Withal praying also for us, that God would open unto us a door of utterance, to speak the mystery of Christ, for which I am also in bonds (Colossians 4:3).

After completing this lesson, the learner will be able to:

1. Recognize that no discipleship efforts are successful without prayer.
2. Analyze Paul's prayer request from the saints.
3. Summarize the importance of prayer before endeavoring to evangelize or disciple others.

Everything begins with prayer! Anything that we purpose to do for the Kingdom of God and Kingdom work must be preceded with communication with the One who has called you to work. The Spirit of the Lord should lead you, guide you, and He will teach you all things. But not only will God lead you, He will strengthen you for the task and give you the anointed word to be used for optimum results.

What's the key to discipleship success and souls maturing as saints of God? Prayer, prayer, and more prayer! Without communication with the Lord through prayer, the results of our efforts at discipleship will be null and void. Jesus says that without Him, you can do nothing. Prayer will always bring the Lord into the situation. Scripture also says that except the Lord builds the house they that labor will labor, but in vain. When you know that God has spoken and is with you, there's no job or task too difficult because the Apostle Paul says that "I can do all things through Christ who strengthens me" (Philippians 4:13).

In today's lesson, the Apostle Paul encourages those in the city of Colossae to pray for his missionary efforts and journey that God would grant them success and give them the words to speak. But the Apostle Paul did not only want to speak mere words, He asked that they pray that his words be seasoned or timely so that it ministers to the needs of everyone that is listening. He knew that his time was limited here on earth just as ours is as well. Thus, he wanted to be effective in preaching the gospel and training those that are new to the faith. But the Apostle Paul knew that his efforts were in vain without prayer.

Remember that prayer opens heaven and prayer pleases God. He knows that you are depending on Him and not on yourself. Prayer also keeps us from being sidetracked because prayer draws you closer to the Lord. What would Nehemiah have done without prayer? Also, look at Hannah's persistence in prayer that brought results. Can we successfully walk in the truth without prayer? Can we successfully disciple others without prayer? Everything we do for the Lord should begin with prayer.

Discussion Questions

1. What is the key for all believers' success in their spiritual walk?
2. What does the Apostle Paul say about the disciples' public life in verses 5-6?
3. What request does the Apostle Paul make of the believers in Colossae in verse 2?

Thought to Remember

Continue in prayer, and watch in the same with thanksgiving! - Colossians 4:2

Lesson 2: Prayer during Discipleship

2 CORINTHIANS 3:5-6; 1 CORINTHIANS 2:3-5
By Freddie and Dianne Campbell

Key Verse: That your faith should not stand in the wisdom of men, but in the power of God (1 Corinthians 2:5).

After completing this lesson, the learner will be able to:

1. Distinguish the purpose of prayer.
2. Identify effective discipleship tools.
3. Build a relationship with the disciple.

Prayer (Hebrew, *Tehinnah*) is essentially a life of communion, a desire to enter into a conscious and intimate relationship with God. Let's look at Matthew 5:6 that states, "Blessed are they which hunger and thirst after righteousness for they shall be filled." A regenerated man, woman, boy, or girl that that has a spiritual rebirth will have a deep hunger and thirst (inner passion and desire to know our Lord and Savior Jesus Christ). Prayer is essential to help fulfill that hunger. Thus, as you disciple a new believer, it is essential that you remind them to: (1) Pray, (2) Fast, and (3) Read God's Word.

Prayer was always a part of the lives of the Old Testament patriarchs and New Testament saints which can be seen in the lives of those such as:

1. Moses - Exodus 32:13
2. Abraham - Genesis 18:22-33
3. Jacob - Genesis 32:24-30
4. David - Psalm 5:3

5. John the Baptist - Luke 11:1
6. Paul - Ephesians 1:15-22

But the most excellent example can be seen in the wonderful book of John chapter 17 where Jesus prayed. It is here that Jesus gave us another example of how to pray as He prayed for Himself to be glorified, the world, and His followers. Likewise, we should pray that God would be glorified through our lives, we should pray for this world, and for all of Jesus' followers. This is because we have more insight than what the Old Testament saints knew which is that God, Jehovah-jireh (The Lord Shall Provide), Jehovah Shammah (The Lord is there), and Jehovah Rohi (The Lord is my Shepherd) is a prayer-answering God (Genesis 22:14) that is able to meet every need that we have as believers.

Likewise, God was able to meet the needs of the Apostle Paul in his weakest moment after much persecution. He realized that it was not his wisdom nor his strength, but the power of God through much prayer, that was able to sustain him on his Christian journey. We must remind new converts and those that are mentoring them that prayer is always important for their growth, development, and maturity.

Discussion Questions

1. Who should we address our prayers to?
2. Why is prayer so important?
3. Why should we always pray before, during, and after mentoring a new convert?

Thought to Remember

Confess your faults one to another, and pray one for another, that you may be healed. The effectual fervent prayer of a righteous man availeth much (James 5:16b).

Lesson 3: Prayer after Discipleship

ACTS 4:31-37

By Donald Lowrance, Jr. and Theresa Lowrance

Key Verse: After they prayed, the place where they were meeting was shaken. And they were all filled with the Holy Spirit and spoke the word of God boldly (Acts 4:31).

After completing this lesson, the learner will be able to:

1. Recognize how God answers prayers today.
2. Describe how God equips followers today to disciple others through prayer.
3. Summarize the significance of the disciples' sharing of their possessions after they had prayer.

We've heard it said time and time again that "Actions speak louder than words". This old idiom can be substantiated in the Word of God. Apostle James let us know that "Faith without works is dead". Our fervent prayers are effectual only through our confidence in the Word of God. The writer of Hebrews tells us that we must first believe that God is (God is who He said He is and is able to do what He said He is able to do). If we meet this prerequisite, then He'll reward those that diligently seek Him. When we pray, we are putting our faith in action. If our requests line up with His divine will, then we should wait in expectation for a manifestation of His holy power through miracles, signs, and wonders.

Our Lord and Savior Jesus Christ is the Author and Finisher of our faith. He is incapable of failure, His every word is true and will never return unto Him void. As followers of Christ, He has already begun a good work in us and promised to perform it until He returns. For those things that God has confirmed in our spirit by the Holy Ghost whether individually or corporately, our will should be to only trust and obey His will and His Word.

In our lesson, the disciples' corporate prayer was a demonstration of the power of God; not only in the midst of the believers, but also unto those that didn't believe. Harmoniously, they prayed unto God through the only name under heaven that can save mankind and that name is Jesus! Not only was their request audible unto men, but most importantly God heard and answered them.

It is worth noting that their prayer made no mention of them selling land, houses, and possessions. So where did this plan originate? It originated in the mind of God. In their day and time, it was God's will for believers to sell all of their possessions and lay it at the Apostles' feet. The Apostles then distributed to every man according to their need. Because of their obedience, they were all blessed and no one was lacking. Is God asking us to sell all of our possessions today? The obvious answer is "No", but it doesn't negate the fact that true believers must work their faith and respond in obedience to God's Word. We can respond to His word by making sure that no believer in God's house is lacking. This can be done through benevolent funds and other means that the church has established for those involved.

Discussion Questions

1. Did God answer His disciples' prayer?
2. How does God equip His disciples?
3. What was the significance of the disciples sharing all that they owned?

Thought to Remember

Through this lesson, we can understand that earthly possessions are temporal, but God's Word is eternal.

Lesson 4: Fasting and Discipleship

1 CORINTHIANS 9:24-27
By Maurice N. Bembry, Sr. and Calvin J. Bembry

Key Verse: And he said unto them, this kind can come forth by nothing, but by prayer and fasting (Mark 9:29).

After completing this lesson, the learner will be able to:

1. Distinguish the purpose of fasting.
2. Identify effective discipleship tools.
3. Build a relationship with the disciple.

Fasting is one of the most misunderstood principles in the Christian faith. Even those in Biblical times such as the Pharisees and Sadducees misapplied and misappropriated the principles and purpose of fasting. Their purpose for fasting was to impress people (Matthew 6:16-18) while others fasted to demonstrate the intensity of their desire to God. Yet others denied themselves to obtain justice as in the case of Mathma Gandhi. All of these are good virtues, but this is not the purpose of fasting.

Isaiah 58:6 asserts that the fasting that God approves of is one that will loose the chains of injustice and untie the cords of the yoke, to set the oppressed free and break every yoke. Thus, the fast is a period of time set aside to afflict our soul, and express true sorrow for sin but it must be accompanied with right motives and the right attitude. Hence, to implement this scripture and to make it relevant for our time, would be fasting so that sinners can be set free as we witness to them and share the gospel (Nehemiah 5:8; Nehemiah 10:31; Ezekiel 18:7). Fasting is essential and vital to discipleship making. We must fast and pray so that the yoke of sin is broken in the lives of those we are witnessing to and mentoring.

Thus, as we share the gospel with others and prepare to disciple them to grow stronger in the Lord after they have been converted, it will require some sacrifices from those doing the witnessing. Now that the disciple is converted they will need your support even more to prevent them from backsliding and leaving the faith. This will require you to humble your soul and body as David did in Psalm 35:13 so that the new convert can remain focused on God. They are not strong enough to fight the enemy, so when you are working with them you should always implement these tools as you witness:

1. Always have a partner.
2. Pray while the other partner speaks.
3. Do not discuss religious denominations.
4. Always let the seeker or new convert read the Bible for themselves.

Even after they are converted, those who are mentoring the disciple should refrain from discussing doctrine. This should be left to their local pastor, Sunday School teacher, discipleship teacher, or Bible Class teacher. Having too many people feeding a new convert or providing the new convert with too much information in the beginning is like trying to feed a new born baby steak and baked potatoes. This is too much meat and food at one time and this will choke the baby. They need milk and they are not prepared to receive so much information after their initial conversion. Just continue to pray with them and encourage them to be faithful to fellowship with the other believers. In time, they too will be mature enough to fast, pray, and witness to others about Jesus.

Discussion Questions

1. Why is important not to provide too much information with new converts?

2. Can you witness and disciple others without fasting? Will it be effective? If so, why or why not?
3. Does your church have a discipleship ministry for new converts? Does your program use a discipleship curriculum? Describe the program.

Thought to Remember

Prayer, fasting, and studying God's Word is vital to get an answer from God! Therefore, we should pray without ceasing (1 Thessalonians 5:17).

Lesson 5: Report and Return to the Mission Field

ACTS 18:12-28
By Luebertha Conner

Key Verse: But bade them farewell...And he sailed from Ephesus. And when he had landed at Caesarea, and gone up, and saluted the church, he went down to Antioch. And after he had spent some time there, he departed, and went over all the country of Galatia and Phrygia in order, strengthening all the disciples (Acts 18: 21-23).

After completing this lesson, the learner will be able to:

1. Prepare to be persecuted for preaching the gospel.
2. Summarize the mission trips of the Apostle Paul during his persecution.
3. Identify new places to preach the gospel as a result of persecution.

After a long and hard day of working, no one wants to come home to complaining kids and a nagging wife. Work alone can be a hostile environment of standoffs and negotiations just to get things done. Thus, when you arrive home you expect to be well-received, loved, and welcomed with open arms.

However, the Apostle Paul was considered a traitor to those in Antioch. It was at Antioch that he persecuted the saints (Acts 11:26). But this was always his home base or home church from whence he departed to preach the gospel. It is in today's lesson that we see a group of Jews got together to start a campaign against the

Apostle Paul and took him into court before the Governor/Deputy of Achaia stirring up trouble for him. But before the Apostle Paul could answer, the case was dismissed because it appeared to be an issue over religious technicality – what is the right way to worship God? For example, there is an old story that says Jesus healed one man's eyes but there are different versions as to how it happened. One man said he healed his eyes with spit and mud (John 9:6), the other with spit and his hands (Mark 8:22-25), and another by faith (Mark 10:46-52). The point is the man was healed and can now see. Let's get down to business about saving souls and winning the lost, not about methods and processes.

Thus, the Apostle Paul left the squabble and went about the Father's business because while they are splitting hairs about religious controversies, souls still needed to be saved. Just like the Apostle Paul took heed to the vision in Acts 16:9 that there stood a man of Macedonia, and prayed him, saying, Come over into Macedonia, and help us.

Likewise, just like he heard the voice of God saying come to Macedonia, I am quite sure he departed from Achaia which was a state where the cities Corinth and Athens abided to travel to Achaia because he saw a need. The Apostle Paul had to return and report to the mission field at the appointed time to meet the servant of the Lord named Apollos.

Apollos was a godly man that knew the scriptures but needed further explanation. This was not a splitting of hairs about methods and processes but obeying God's Word. He only knew of the baptism of John, but they explained to Him the full story about repentance and baptism in the name of Jesus to have His sins remitted and removed. The knowledge of repentance is good. Godly sorrow leads to repentance but once you repent you must have your sins removed and receive God's power to continue to live a godly life and to be His witness. Believers are saved for no other reason but to be a witness for Christ and bring Him Glory. The witness may be on the mission field, your neighborhood, your job, or your home. Know that you will suffer persecution but day by day you must return and report to the mission field.

Discussion Questions

1. Should we be afraid to preach the gospel because of persecution (Acts 18:12-17)?
2. Where do we go and who do we run to when we are persecuted?
3. Should we leave the mission field or travel to another place to preach the gospel when we are not well received in one location? Why or Why not? (Acts 18:24-28)

Thought to Remember

Listen to the voice of God to serve the souls that need us and go wherever He leads us.

UNIT 11: MEETING THE NEEDS OF DISCIPLES

Lesson 1: Pray for Deliverance

ACTS 16:16-24
By Betty J. Hunn

Key Verse: And this did she many days. But Paul, being grieved, turned and said to the spirit, I command thee in the name of Jesus Christ to come out of her. And he came out the same hour (Acts 16:18).

After completing this lesson, the learner will be able to:

1. Recognize and discern the signs that an individual needs to be delivered from sin.
2. Identify the sources and problems that may keep the individual bound in sin.
3. Examine the avenues and support mechanisms that will keep the individual delivered from sin.

Today's lesson shares the story of a young woman possessed with a spirit of witchcraft that brought her masters much gain. She followed the Apostle Paul many days and he turned to the spirit and commanded that the spirit in the name of Jesus to come out. Her masters were upset because their gains were now gone. They brought it to the attention of the magistrate and Paul and Silas were thrown in jail.

Thus, when we are witnessing to others on the mission field within our communities, jobs, and even overseas, there will be individuals that need to be delivered. They may be possessed with the spirit of witchcraft or fortune telling or they may have other spirit possessions. They could be addicted to drugs and alcohol, liars, thieves, prostitutes and exotic dancers, jealous, bitter, those that seek to divide, or other types of spirits that all come from

141

Satan. Anything that is not a characteristic of the fruit of the Spirit and that is contrary to God and His Word is from the devil.

Therefore, as we witness to individuals and begin to teach them God's Word, we must pray that they are delivered from whatever sin or demonic spirit is influencing their lives. We must pray for them to stop listening to the voices that tell them to disobey God's Word. Sometimes the voice telling them to disobey God might be their employer (pimp, drug king pin, witch, warlock, etc.) who will be upset that they no longer work for them. Their enslavement to the drug habit or prostitution keeps their pockets full of money. In addition, others may be upset that they no longer receive funds to counsel them for drug addiction, depression, or the business owner that has lost his best exotic dancer or prostitute. No matter who gets upset about the individual's deliverance, they still need to be set free from the bondage of sin. Jesus came to seek and to save those who are lost not to help sinners continue to get rich off of those who are bound.

Discussion Questions

1. Can you name individuals who are bound by sin that you have not witnessed to? Have you prayed for their deliverance?
2. As you review the story of the woman possessed with a spirit of witchcraft and those who stood to gain from her divination, how would you confront and handle those who tried to hinder you from helping those who are bound that you have witnessed to?
3. Are you willing to go to jail (like Paul) for helping someone be set free from their captors and the captive of sin?

Thought to Remember

If you call upon the name of the Lord, He will deliver you!

Lesson 2: Pray for Healing

ACTS 3 & ACTS 4
By Wanda E. Burton and Barbara Brown

Key Verse: By stretching forth thine hand to heal; and that signs and wonders may be done by the name of thy holy child Jesus (Acts 4:30).

After completing this lesson, the learner will be able to:

1. Identify the signs and wonders that accompany the healing name of Jesus.
2. Examine the acts of the Apostles in the book of Acts.
3. Demonstrate and exercise the same authority as Jesus and the Apostles through God's Word.

After Jesus had ascended into the heavens, His disciples who were followers of the teachings of Jesus Christ, were still obedient and used their lives as a testimony. They were great examples of Jesus' teachings because they lived a life that was pleasing unto Him and a life that was obedient to the teachings found in the Word of God. It was because of their obedience to the scriptures and their godly lifestyle, that the signs and wonders would follow them. Mark 16:17-18 says *"And these signs shall follow them that believe; In my name shall they cast out devils; they shall speak with new tongues; They shall take up serpents; and if they drink any deadly thing, it shall not hurt them; they shall lay hands on the sick, and they shall recover."*

Thus, in Acts chapter 3 we see that Peter and John, the disciples of Jesus, were on their way to the temple to pray. These disciples had faith and obedience to Acts 2:38-47. They demonstrated their faith by obeying the scripture found in Luke 18:1 which says that "men ought always pray and not faint". So, as they approached the temple they saw the man that was lame who was unable to walk sitting by the gate called *Beautiful*. He would always ask those entering and exiting the temple for alms and charitable gifts.

Peter and John let the lame man know that they did not have the alms or money that he was asking for but that they were willing to share with the lame man what they had. The lame man was told in the name of Jesus Christ of Nazareth "rise up and walk". Just like the lame man needed help, sometimes we need help as well, so Peter and John took the lame man by the hand and lifted him up. As the lame man stood, God performed a miracle because of Peter and John's faith and strengthened the man's ankle bones.

The lame man was so appreciative about his healing that as he entered the temple, he began to leap and give God praise and thanks for his healing. Everyone in the temple knew who he was because the lame man had been sitting at the gate called *Beautiful* for years. They knew about his previous condition and how he had been begging and asking people for money. But this time, God met the lame man's need in a different way.

Often times as we pray for one another, whether it's for spiritual healing or physical healing, there may be other things that they need as well. Money can't buy healing, but the prayers of the righteous avails much. Thus as we pray for one another, we know that God is able to heal, but other times God may give us grace to endure the afflictions until He returns or until we fall asleep in Jesus. Jesus is a healer and He always heals on time. Remember that our help is in the Lord who made heaven and earth, according to Psalm 124:8.

Thus, we the saints of the living God when praying for others' healings sometimes we have to intercede for them. They may not have the faith, knowledge, or understanding that Jesus is going to heal them regardless of their condition. Today so many people suffer from diseases of the mind, such as bipolar disorder and schizophrenia, along with afflictions of the heart, soul, and spirit. We have to pray and ask Jesus to touch their mind and to heal them. Just as Peter and John saw the lame man at the temple asking for alms; they did not give him what he asked for, but they gave him what he needed. They had to pray and believe God for his healing.

Therefore, we have to be bold like Peter and John and meet the needs of others and to pray and have faith for others to be healed in their mind, body, soul, and spirit. We must always remind them that it is Jesus who healed them and that we were just a vessel to pray and intercede on their behalf.

Discussion Questions

1. After reading Acts 3 and Acts 4 name some of the signs and wonders that the apostles rendered in the name of Jesus.
2. Does God hear the sinner's prayer? Is it only for repentance or can it be for healing and other things?
3. When and how does a believer receive the same power and authority that Jesus and the apostles had?

Thought to Remember

God is the healer and man is just a vessel that God uses in the process!

Lesson 3: Prepare them a Meal

MATTHEW 14:10-21
By Barbara Rusan

Key Verse: But Jesus said unto them, They need not depart; give ye them to eat (Matthew 14:16).

After completing this lesson, the learner will be able to:

1. Recognize the importance of meeting the natural and spiritual needs of disciples.
2. Distinguish between natural need and spiritual need.
3. Discover the importance of relying on the Holy Spirit to meet the needs of disciples.

In this discourse, Jesus was demonstrating a powerful lesson that the disciples had yet to learn. They were always quick to send people away empty regardless to what the need was. For example, the mother who needed help they wanted to send her away, the children that wanted to touch Jesus they also wanted to send away, and those who were hungry and following Jesus in today's lesson, they wanted to send them away.

However, Jesus was a man full of compassion. He practiced mercy and love to any lost soul. He always wanted to minister to the total person - the mind, body, soul, and spirit. No matter what Jesus had going on, He put the needs of others first. Just like in today's lesson, history tells us that Jesus was dealing with the death of his cousin (John the Baptist) but he denied his emotions and was compelled with compassion to meet the needs of the multitude by healing the sick (natural) and feeding/teaching them the Word of God (spiritual).

But once he was done taking care of their natural and spiritual needs, another situation arose as they prepared to travel to the other side to rest. Some of the followers had their natural (healing) and spiritual needs (Word of God) met while others were yet lacking. The disciples were tired and wanted to rest and send the followers away. But Jesus admonished them not to send the disciples away because there was still a natural need (food) and a spiritual need (unbelief). They'd heard the teaching but were not quite sure they accepted and believed all that He said. Thus, Jesus said, bring them to Me.

As they returned to Jesus, He commanded them to sit down and He blessed the food (five loaves and two fishes) as He looked towards heaven. He was setting an example that all our help comes from the Lord, the Maker of heaven and earth. After He blessed the food, the disciples distributed the food to about five thousand men, not including the women and children. The Lord performed that miracle and met their spiritual and natural needs. They were spiritually fed by driving out doubt (whether or not He was God) and they were naturally fed with the food.

As believers, we should know that no matter what we are going through as a saint of God, we have to look to God in prayer and put our problems aside and see the needs of the people. We need to spiritually discern when they are hurting, depressed, hungry, addicted to drugs and alcohol, and whether they are homeless or just need our help. People need to be fed spiritually and naturally. Just as Jesus laid aside His own needs to minister to others, we should do likewise.

Discussion Questions

1. If you had to feed a large crowd of more than 5,000 people what would you serve? How would you serve them?

2. Most churches forget the impossible, leaving out faith and trust; therefore they fail to meet the spiritual and natural needs of the lost. What are some things your church can do?
3. What do you think about Jesus' reaction to the death of his cousin John the Baptist? How would you handle such news after being besieged with meeting the needs of others?

Thought to Remember

Then he said to him, "a certain man gave a great supper and invited many, and he sent his servant at supper time to say to these who were invited, "Come, for all things are ready" (Luke 14:16-17 NKJV).

Lesson 4: Meetings That Matter

LUKE 19:1-10
By Gerald W. Ledford, Sr. and Evelyn Ledford

Key Verse: And when Jesus came to the place, he looked up, and saw him, and said unto him, Zacchaeus, make haste, and come down; for today I must abide at thy house (Luke 19:5).

After completing this lesson, the learner will be able to:

1. Demonstrate the love of Christ to a hostile world when witnessing.
2. Identify the fears he/she faces in witnessing to others.
3. Analyze the juxtaposition for evangelism.

Today's lesson endeavors to remind, support, and encourage those who evangelize to keep their ministry assignments and appointments. It is easy to become discouraged and to cancel speaking engagements or individual meetings with sinners and saints. We think "Well, they really don't want to hear what I have to say" or "I have witnessed to them so many times before and the message is never well received". But as we look at the example of Jesus in this passage we saw that He did not fail to keep His individual appointment with a tax collector named Zacchaeus.

In our modern times, we would call this a Jabez appointment (1 Chronicles 4:9-10). As Jesus entered Jericho and was passing through, a man was there by the name of Zacchaeus, a wealthy chief tax collector. Tax Collectors during the Ancient Roman time period were men hired by the government to collect taxes from all citizens and men working in the Roman Empire. If the tax collector could get more than the person owed the government, the tax collector was able to keep the extra money. This is why tax collectors were not liked by many people - they were considered greedy and dishonest.

But Zacchaeus had a change of heart when Jesus came to town. Zacchaeus wanted to see who Jesus was, but because he was short, he could not see over the crowd so he ran ahead and climbed up a sycamore tree to see Him. Oh, how his life changed when he met Jesus. When Jesus came to the place, he looked up and said to Zacchaeus "come down" that he must visit at his house today. Zacchaeus came down at once and welcomed Jesus joyfully.

When all the people saw that, they began to murmur, saying Jesus was going to be the guest of a sinner. Zacchaeus told the Lord if he had cheated anyone out of anything, he would pay back four times the amount. Jesus told him that "today", salvation had come to his house because he belongs to the family of Abraham. Jesus came to seek and to save the lost. Zacchaeus received more than he could ever think because of the meeting with Jesus. Something happens to each person who meets Jesus. For example, Blind Bartimaeus' eyes were opened when he met Jesus (Luke 18:35-43). Another divine or Jabez appointment was the woman with the issue of blood, who was made whole when she met Jesus (Mark 5:25-34, Luke 8:43-48). Lastly, the ten lepers were healed when they met Jesus (Luke 17:11-19).

All of these encounters should encourage us as ministers, missionaries, and evangelists because we see that if we would bring someone to Jesus or bring Jesus through the preached Word to another individual or nation, their lives would change too. Just as with Zacchaeus, God loves us no matter what mistakes we have made, we must trust in the Lord (Proverbs 3:5-6, Psalm 37:3-5). Jesus is standing at the door of your heart knocking, all we have to do is keep the appointment and allow Him to come into our heart (Revelation 3:20-22). Jesus' arms are wide open to receive all that will meet Him.

Discussion Questions

1. Discuss the press Zacchaeus had to meet Jesus.
2. Discuss the results of the press of Zacchaeus.
3. Are you ready to meet Jesus? Do you know those that are not ready to meet Jesus and have you scheduled an appointment to meet with them?

Thought to Remember

Jesus loves us no matter what mistakes we have made!

UNIT 12: MAKING DISCIPLES

Lesson 1: Discipleship and Obedience

ECCLESIASTES 12:13; LUKE 6:45-49; JOHN 8:31
By Sandra D. Walker

> *Key Verse: And he that sent me is with me: the Father hath not left me alone; for I do always those things that please him (John 8:29).*

After completing this lesson, the learner will be able to:

1. Recognize the importance of total obedience to God.
2. Demonstrate, by example, true discipleship.
3. Identify some of the pitfalls of disobedience.

As we look at mainstream Christianity, everyone is so apt to say they are doing the will of the Father and yet they live a life that pleases oneself, predominately the flesh. Man's own wisdom, knowledge, and excuses dictate his thinking that it's not necessary to deny yourself completely but rather just to succumb to some biblical principles and become a follower of Christ. However, Jesus while in preparation for the cross, admonished His followers and disciples that if they love Him they were to keep His commandments (John 14:15) and to do the will of the One who sent Him (John 6:38). The word "disciple" means one who adheres to His teaching and teaches others to do the same.

Strong's Complete Dictionary of the Bible states that the Greek definition of "obedience" is **(hupakouó) hoop-ak-oo'-o** meaning "submission". The Hebrew word **(shama) shaw-mah'** means "to hear intelligently or give ear". Simply put, it is imperative that a disciple become disciplined by submission and he/she must be able to hear intelligently. As we align ourselves with the word of God, we realize that no matter what our status in life may be with its twists, challenges, losses, and victories, as we search for a meaningful and fulfilling life we realize that it can only come through obedience to God. Thus, one is never to lose sight of the very essence of being created to reverence and glorify Him graciously and wholeheartedly to do His will. This is the sole purpose of man's existence.

The Apostle Paul in the book of Romans considered himself a servant of Jesus Christ and as a servant he recognized he needed to be obedient at all costs. He also admonished Christians and reminded them that they were more than conquerors through Him that loved us (Romans 8:37-39). He did not allow anything to hinder his walk and we must have that same vigor and tenacity of those before us because they left us a great legacy. Throughout the Bible, the mandate for obedience has been paramount and the consequences for disobedience are clear (Genesis 2:16-17; Deuteronomy 32:51-52; John 4:34; and Revelation 3:21).

Naturally speaking, a tree is known by the fruit it bears and how much more than for the child of God. Therefore, if being led by the Spirit of God one can only produce good fruit, then one's mind, actions, faculties, conversation, and character must and will be in divine submission. Though storms, floods, tsunamis, test, trials, and tribulations come, we should not be moved for we rest on the promises of God (Isaiah 59:19b). Remember we are kept by the power of God (1 Peter 1:5).

On the downside of this, those that choose to remain and walk in carnality or the flesh by resurrecting the old man, what right do they have to call God our Father, their Father? Their demise is inevitable for they shall be beaten with many stripes (Luke 12:47). So as we continually strive to please the Master and walk in obedience as dear children know with certainty that a righteous crown awaits you.

Discussion Questions

1. What are some of the hindrances in your life that you have identified that are causing you not to obey God?
2. Why do you think the Apostles were so adamant about proclaiming the gospel of Jesus Christ?
3. What steps can you make in your local assembly to bring about change, being adamant about proclaiming the gospel of Jesus Christ?

Thought to Remember

A tree's roots are as deep as the nourishment it receives. What's nourishing your roots?

Lesson 2: Terms of Discipleship

LUKE 9:57-62
By Niares A. Hunn

> *Key Verse: And Jesus said unto him, No man, having put his hand to the plough, and looking back, is fit for the kingdom of God (Luke 9:62).*

After completing this lesson, the learner will be able to:

1. Compare and contrast terms of discipleship versus cost of discipleship.
2. Examine three discipleship applications.
3. Value the terms of discipleship.

Definitions are very important points of clarification to make sure that words are being used correctly, and it helps the reader understand the precise message that is being communicated. Words have meaning and we must understand that we are to assume responsibility for using them. For example, when you buy a new home or car, you sign a contract to agree to the terms and conditions. The term is usually 60 months (5 years) or 72 months (6 years) for the car and 15 or 30 years for the home. The conditions as to whether you get to keep the home or car are based on things such as (1) maintenance, (2) payments, and (3) taxes, registrations, etc. But these are merely terms and conditions that you count up as you endeavor to make this sacrifice.

Marriage also has some terms and conditions that we assume as we partake of the marriage vows. We agree to forsake all others, we agree to love them in sickness and health, "until death do us part". These are all terms that we agree to when we assume the responsibility of marriage. Thus far, we have been discussing the parameters of the word "terms" by using examples such as marriage and purchases without providing a specific definition. Terms are for a fixed or limited period of time for which something is intended to last such as car payments 5 or 6 years, homes loans 15 or 30 years, and marriage indefinitely.

Although the cost (financial investment and/or time spent) may vary, the sacrifice depends on the terms that were agreed to. For example, you can re-negotiate the terms for the car payment or mortgage by moving the due date, skipping a payment, and adding it to the end of the loan, or getting a lower interest rate. Likewise, in marriage you can re-negotiate the premarital counseling vows or terms from one child to three children that was agreed upon or that the wife stays at home to care for the house to the terms of her working part time to help meet family expenses.

All of these are important examples regarding our lesson today. We know that salvation is a free gift, but it did not come cheap. Jesus Christ sacrificed His own life and shed His blood to provide salvation for us. This cost Jesus His life so that we might have eternal life. Although salvation is not for sale, when we accept Jesus Christ as our Lord and Savior, we are agreeing to the terms and conditions of dying to our lives, ways, and habits and we become alive in Him (Galatians 2:20).

Thus, in our lesson today Jesus had three applicants or three people that wanted to be His disciples. In verses 57-58, we have the hasty disciple, in verses 59-60 the procrastinating disciple, and lastly in verses 61-62 the disciple who was indecisive, wavering and had unresolved issues. As we examine these three applicants, each wanted discipleship on their terms and conditions. As an altar worker, you will see people that come to the altar crying, with looks of despair, or with a gleam of excitement in their eyes, each desiring to follow Jesus. But when the altar worker discusses the terms of salvation such as (1) this is a life-changing decision (2) repentance is necessary (3) baptism is required, and (4) The Holy Spirit is essential; sometimes the response becomes well not today

I just want prayer. Others might reply have replied well I will get baptized today, but I don't want to repent or receive the Holy Ghost.

This response is surprising and makes one think they were just moved by the message and excited about what they heard but not ready to agree to the terms of the message. Instead, their response becomes I want Jesus on my terms and my way. I want the social gospel or want to join the church social club to mark on my Facebook page that I checked in at Mt. Zion Church today. I have done the church thing today or this week...now on with the rest of my life. I checked into church today like it's a job and now I am checking out because it's 12 pm or 1 pm. See you next week Jesus.

However, we need to understand that our relationship with Jesus exists every day. When we have (1) repented, (2) been baptized in the name of Jesus Christ for the remission of our sins, and (3) received the Holy Spirit which is Christ in you; then Jesus is with you every day. He lives in you so this becomes a lifetime commitment. We are no longer our own (1 Corinthians 6:19-20). Our desire should be to spend time with Him each day in His Word and to spend time with Him more than once a week on Sundays. We should want to give up our old life and now we live for Him and spend time at Bible class, Women's Retreat, Men's Prayer Meeting and other church-related activities to grow and mature in our relationship with Him.

Thus, we cannot be hasty in our decision to follow Christ (Luke 9:57-58) but we must count up the cost and once we evaluate and agree to what is being asked of us, then we should make our calling and election sure. Also, we cannot procrastinate and think we have time to make a decision. Jesus is coming soon and tomorrow is not promised to us. We can't think we have time to plan a three or seven day funeral (Luke 9:59-60), time to party, time to travel, or do those last minute things before we go to the marriage supper while the bridegroom waits (Matthew 22:1-14; Luke 14:16-24; Revelation 19:6-9). We must have the oil (the Holy Spirit) living inside of our vessels and be ready when Jesus comes as the songwriter has stated.

Lastly, we cannot be indecisive and halting between two opinions of whether we will serve the Lord or continue to follow Satan. The applicant in Luke 9:61-62 had some unresolved issues and was indecisive about whether he wanted to follow Jesus Christ now or get his family's approval and tell them "goodbye" before he followed Jesus as a disciple. We have to be like Lot (Genesis 19:26) and let go of the world, our wife, husband, or families as we decide to follow Jesus Christ and accept the terms and approval. The scripture lets us know that Lot continued on the journey because he did not look back and become a pillar of salt; instead the scripture declares in Genesis 19:30 that Lot and his daughters were living in a cave in the mountains. Just as Abraham had to leave his kindred and follow God (Genesis 12:1; Acts 7:3), you and I must make this same decision and declaration, I have decided to follow Jesus, no turning back.

Discussion Questions

1. Share your salvation story and what brought you to the saving knowledge of Jesus Christ.
2. When you initially got saved, were the terms and conditions explained to you or did you learn about this later after attending church services?
3. Do you think that the terms of discipleship should be explained up front or after an individual has been saved?

Thought to Remember

I have decided to follow Jesus;
I have decided to follow Jesus;
I have decided to follow Him;
No turning back, no turning back.

Lesson 3: Cost of Discipleship

LUKE 14:25-34
By Helen J. Thomas

Key Verse: If any man come to me, and hate not his father, and mother, and wife, and children, and brethren, and sisters, yea, and his own life also, he cannot be my disciple. Herein is my Father glorified, that ye bear much fruit; so shall ye be my disciples (Luke 14:26).

After completing this lesson, the learner will be able to:

1. Identify the requirements of being a disciple.
2. Examine the cost of being a disciple.
3. Prepare to totally commit your life to Christ.

Many people were following after Jesus. Yet Jesus is telling the people that they must love Him more than they love anyone. This means you must love Jesus more than you love your father, mother, wife, husband, children, sister, or brother. Jesus uses this example because even in today's society everyone loves their family and places a high value on their kinfolk. People draw the line when others seek to offend their loved ones because they love their family and want to protect them at all costs. But Jesus is saying you must love Me more than you love your kinfolk and even yourself. We see this example when God asked Abraham to sacrifice his only son Isaac. But look at God's response to Abraham because of his sacrifice in Genesis 22:12: *And he said, Lay not thine hand upon the lad, neither do thou anything unto him: for now I know that thou fearest God, seeing thou hast not withheld thy son, thine only son from me.* This is saying that you not only fear God but you love God. You

162

love and fear God so much that you are going to sacrifice your only son for Him.

Just as Abraham was willing to make a sacrifice for God, Jesus sacrificed Himself for us to have a relationship with Him. Jesus is asking every believer to count up the cost in this manner as pointed out in our lesson today:

1. Hate our families and ourselves (verse 26)
2. Carry our own cross (verse 27)
3. Give up all our possessions (verse 33)

Thus, Jesus is saying if you plan to build a tower you first would have to figure out the cost to see if you can afford it and have the money to complete. You consider how much it will cost to build this tower so that you are not scorned by others because you could not finish building the tower. Likewise, you will be scorned by your family, friends, co-workers, and enemies if you start out in the Christian race and decide to return to the world. They will mock you and say, "I knew that they were not going to continue to follow Jesus. I knew that they would go back to fornication, lying, stealing, drinking, partying, using vulgar language, hatred, jealousy, and other sinful practices."

Remember no man having put his hand to the plow and looking back is fit for the kingdom of God (Luke 9:62). Always keep your eyes on Jesus the author and finisher of your faith. Let the scoffers and mockers do their job and you live godly because all those that live godly will suffer persecution (2 Timothy 3:12). Never take your eyes off the prize as you consider and count up the cost. Remember now unto him who is able to keep you from falling and to present you faultless before the presence of his glory with exceeding joy (Jude 1:24). It gives God great joy when you consider and count the cost of being His disciple by allowing Him to present you faultless just as He asked Satan, "Have you considered by servant Job?" What has God told Satan about you? Have you considered <u>Your Name in the Blank</u>?

Discussion Questions

1. How does "carrying your cross" relate to "hating your own life" so that you can be His disciple?
2. Why does Luke include the Parable of Building the Tower and Assessing Military Strength in relations to being Jesus' disciples (14:28-30)?
3. Putting things in perspective, how does Jesus' words about "giving up everything he has" have to do with owning a house and car? With purchasing a refrigerator? With seeking an academic degree? Do we have to forsake these things also to be Jesus' disciple?

Thought to Remember

Salvation is a free gift but it cost Jesus the sacrifice of His life!

Lesson 4: Disciples Bear Fruit

JOHN 15:1-8
By Jonathan W. Hunn, Sr.

Key Verse: Herein is my Father glorified, that ye bear much fruit; so shall ye be my disciples (John 15:8).

After completing this lesson, the learner will be able to:

1. Define the husbandman, vine, and branches.
2. Examine the criteria for bearing fruit.
3. Recognize the purpose of bearing fruit.

Is it surprising to know that receiving the Holy Spirit alone doesn't necessarily result in the fruit of the Spirit being manifested in our lives? It is our relationship with Christ that determines how much fruit we bring forth. John 15:4 says, "Abide in me, and I in you. As the branch cannot bear fruit of itself, except it abide in the vine; no more can ye, except ye abide in me." There are certain criteria that must be established to allow fruit to be brought forth in our lives. The first criterion to bear fruit is you must be connected to the vine, the Lord Jesus Christ.

How can you produce anything without being connected to the source of power such as "the vine?" It is impossible. Just like a lamp cannot work unless it too is connected to its source of power. Certainly, the first step to any individual bringing forth fruit or spiritual attributes is being connected to the source, which is Christ. John 15:3 proclaims that you must be clean through the word of God and Psalm 119:11 says, "Thy word have I hid in my heart that I may not sin against you." Sin causes stagnation and prevents any individual from bearing fruit and living up to their spiritual potential.

Any natural branch that does not bear fruit needs to be pruned or cut off. Scripture states that a dead branch is not useful so it is cut off and thrown out. We as Christians must inspect ourselves so we may rid ourselves of our dead branches or any dead weight. Hebrews 12:1 admonishes us to lay aside every weight, and the sin that doth so easily beset us. Dead branches can't bear fruit. Only those branches that are alive and well bear good fruit.

If we abide in Christ and His Word abides in us, then we have the elements or formula to be both a spiritual and natural success; because of this, the fruit that we bear from our branches will show forth the characteristics of Christ shown through us. Every word that we speak, every endeavor and every action will be a reflection of the Christ who lives in us.

Discussion Questions

1. What is the duty of the husbandman, vine, and branch?
2. Have you experienced God's pruning in your life? How did this make you feel?
3. Are you still bearing fruit in your life today? How?

Thought to Remember

Verily, verily, I say unto you, except a corn of wheat fall into the ground and die, it abideth alone: but if it dies, it bringeth forth much fruit (John 12:24).

Printed in the United States
By Bookmasters